EVERY CHILD READY FOR SCHOOL

EVERY CHILD READY FOR SCHOOL

HELPING ADULTS INSPIRE YOUNG CHILDREN TO LEARN

Dorothy Stoltz • Elaine M. Czarnecki • Connie Wilson

ala
editions

AN IMPRINT OF THE AMERICAN LIBRARY ASSOCIATION
CHICAGO • 2013

Dorothy Stoltz coordinates outreach services and programming at Carroll County (Maryland) Public Library. She spearheaded a successful early literacy training research study, which showed statistically significant increases in early literacy skills of children. With more than twenty-five years of experience in public libraries, she oversees early literacy training, peer coaching, programming, mobile services, community outreach, and grant projects, including "Parents as Teachers," at her library. She is the author of several articles in professional journals. In 2011 she became a member of the ALSC/PLA Every Child Ready to Read Oversight Committee. She earned her MLS at Clarion University of Pennsylvania.

Elaine M. Czarnecki is a literacy consultant with the firm Resources in Reading in Annapolis, Maryland. She teaches for Johns Hopkins University and is a former elementary school–based reading specialist. She provides professional development in the area of emergent literacy to children's librarians across Maryland and has given similar workshops in Virginia, Pennsylvania, Wisconsin, and Minnesota. Since 2001 she has provided consulting services for a variety of library initiatives, including the Emergent Literary Training Assessment Project. She has coauthored two articles for *Public Libraries*. She earned her master's degree in education with a concentration in reading at Loyola University in Maryland.

Connie Wilson recently retired after twenty-one years in librarian and supervisory positions at Carroll County (Maryland) Public Library. Her original career encompassed ten years of social work in New York. Moving to Maryland, Connie returned to her first love—libraries. She brought her social work experience, work with children, and trainer certification to her library positions. Connie has led various literacy workshops for parents, child care professionals, and librarians in Virginia and Pennsylvania. She was the lead program trainer for Maryland and Delaware Library Associate Trainees. She is a national and international conference presenter and has coauthored two articles for *Public Libraries*.

Printed in the United States of America

17   16   15   14   13   5   4   3   2   1

Extensive effort has gone into ensuring the reliability of the information in this book; however, the publisher makes no warranty, express or implied, with respect to the material contained herein.

ISBNs: 978-0-8389-1125-9 (paper); 978-0-8389-9660-7 (PDF).

Library of Congress Cataloging-in-Publication Data
Stoltz, Dorothy.
    Every child ready for school : helping adults inspire young children to learn / Dorothy Stoltz, Elaine
    M. Czarnecki, and Connie Wilson.
       pages   cm
    Includes bibliographical references and index.
    ISBN 978-0-8389-1125-9
    1. Libraries and caregivers—United States—Case studies. 2. Libraries and preschool children—United States—Case studies. 3. Readiness for school—United States—Case studies. 4. Child care workers—Training of—United States—Case studies. 5. Early childhood education—Parent participation—United States—Case studies. 6. Preschool children—Books and reading—United States. 7. Carroll County Public Library. I. Czarnecki, Elaine M. II.
    Wilson, Connie, 1946- III. Title.
    Z711.92.C37S76 2012
    025.5'6—dc23   2012027259

Cover design by Kirstin Krutsch. Images © Shutterstock, Inc.
Text design by Mary Bowers in the Archer and Verlag typefaces.

♾ This paper meets the requirements of ANSI/NISO Z39.48-1992 (Permanence of Paper).

In memory of my parents, Walter Stoltz and Margaret Bobak Stoltz, who inspired me to learn.

—DOROTHY

In memory of my mother, Julie Price, who surrounded me with books and love and made visits to the public library a special outing for me as a child.

—ELAINE

For all adults who take seriously their responsibility to help children develop and thrive on their way to school readiness, and for my granddaughter, Eloise Jean.

—CONNIE

Contents

 Downloadable versions of the material listed can be found at www.alaeditions.org/webextras

Preface

We'd like to introduce you to two four-year-olds. Think about the similarities and differences in their day with their child care provider.

Our first child is Sam. Sam enters his child care home at 7 o'clock in the morning. His child care provider, Ms. Molly, greets him with a smile. He goes into the living room, where cartoons are already on the television. He sits down with a couple of other children to watch them. Sam and the other children have snacks, and then they play outside for a while. They lunch at the kitchen table, take a nap, and then watch a video in the afternoon. Sam's mom picks him up at 5 p.m. He hugs her and waves good-bye to Ms. Molly as they leave.

Our second child is Thomas. Thomas enters his child care home at 7 o'clock in the morning. His child care provider, Ms. Katie, greets him with a smile. She says they will be discussing birds today and asks him what birds he likes. Thomas says he sees a lot of robins and blue jays, but he really likes to see ducks and geese on the water. As they walk to the playroom with the other children, she listens attentively and asks him to compare robins, blue jays, ducks, and geese. In the playroom are baskets of books, building blocks, a play store, puppets, and a science table, which this week has a display of fall leaves and acorns from their nature walk.

Ms. Katie starts the day with a discussion about several kinds of birds. She takes the children outside to look for birds in the sky, trees, and yard. Thomas likes it when she asks questions. He feels encouraged to talk about the birds he sees and hears. He is excited to see a duck next door and imitates the way she walks and screeches "Quack, quack, qu-u-a-a-a-a-a-a-a-ck." When they go inside, Ms. Katie shares two new books with the children. One of the stories, *Make Way for Ducklings*, the children especially relate to because of the duck next door. Ms. Katie also introduces them to a nonfiction book about common birds they might see. The children can talk about the bird when they see a picture they recognize. Thomas sees a robin and tells everyone he saw one at his sister's bus stop yesterday. Ms. Katie sings several songs with them, plays a rhyming game, and involves the children in telling a flannelboard story about ducks. They finish the morning with an art project to make a bird.

They have snacks and lunch and then take naps. In the afternoon, the library van visits and the children tell the librarian about the birds they've seen and the duck next door. The librarian shares a short-themed storytime that includes several picture books, songs, and a fingerplay. After the children sing the ending song, they go with Ms. Katie to choose books from the library van. She lets each child select two or three books that they are interested in while she works with the librarian to find appropriate books for her future themes. After a short quiet time while the children look at the books they selected from the library van, Ms. Katie sets up an indoor activity because it has started to rain. The children enjoy an active game of following directions by crawling, walking, and hopping through a maze Ms. Katie has created with tables, chairs, boxes, and blocks. They then have free play in the activity centers and the book area until time to go home.

Thomas's mom picks him up at 5 p.m. Ms. Katie gives her a handout with the words to the songs they sang along with the titles of the books the children read with her that day. Thomas excitedly tells his mom everything he's learned about ducks. He tells her that he wants to read one of his picture books about ducks in the car. He waves and tells Ms. Katie good-bye as they leave.

Both children have a kind child care provider, but in the first instance she is little more than a babysitter, in the second instance, a caring education professional.

❈

To encourage and motivate child care providers to inspire children to learn, Carroll County (Maryland) Public Library conducted a scientific research study and training program. We offered the trainings to professionals first and then to parents to help them create environments with age-appropriate books, play materials, and opportunities for young children to explore and learn. This book is a record of these programs and a guide for offering the training in your own community.

Everyone knows that children are inherently inquisitive. They want to know things and ask many questions. To be successful in life, it is important to ask intelligent questions and be able to figure out the answers. It is important to think clearly, to discern your limitations and overcome them. The role of adults is to provide guidance and point children in the right direction.

Libraries have an incredible role in helping children develop a lifelong enjoyment of learning. The power of the library is that it can provide most of the answers for children through books and other learning platforms. The library is a vast resource of information.

Libraries are redefining themselves in a rapidly changing world. Our school readiness training is an example of how a library can increase its role as a valuable community resource. The goal is to motivate adults to inspire young children to learn.

Training adults to promote school readiness in a playful, language rich environment is a joyful experience. We hope to convey some of this joy to you as you read about our initiative.

Acknowledgments

We have had the privilege of working with many of the finest child care professionals, parents, library staff, and community partners, and we thank those we have worked with who shared our passion for helping children become ready for school. We gratefully acknowledge and express deep appreciation to the many wonderful people who have made this project possible:

- to our workshop participants (especially, Erin Mullinix, Karen Kanagy, Patti Green, Yahaira Zurira, and Emma Bartow), whose deep sharing and insight have moved us many levels beyond our own thinking

- to our colleagues, including Dianne Black, Peg Pond, Kelley Gordon, Kris Holocker, Marie Speck, Lynda Gainor, Barbara Summers, Denise Magee, Elena Hartley, and Martha Portocarrero, for their significant reflections and contributions

- to Stephanie Shauck, Kathleen Reif, Gail Griffith, Saroj Ghoting, Gilda Martinez, Carl Japikse, Robert Leichtman, Sarah Long, Betsy Diamant-Cohen, Marisa Conner, Linda Mielke, Steven Herb, Julie Rinehart, Susan Roberts, Rich Bowra, and Susan Mitchell, for their wisdom and inspiration

- to Irene Padilla, Daria Parry, Paula Isett, Susan Paznekas, and everyone at the Maryland State Department of Education Division of Library Development and Services and the Institute for Museum and Library Services, for their encouragement, guidance, and funding that made the research study possible

- to Louise Corwin at Ready At Five, for her above-and-beyond support

- to our associates at the Maryland State Department of Education, especially Nancy Grasmick, Rolf Grafwallner, Elizabeth Kelley, Valerie Kaufman, and Cheryl DeAtley, for their early learning vision and project blessing

- to our friends in the Carroll County Family Child Care Association, Carroll County Early Childhood Consortium, Carroll County Public Schools, Carroll County Local Management Board, the Judith P. Hoyer Early Child Care and Education Enhancement Program (our "Judy Center"), and the "Parents as Teachers" collaboration, including Joyce Tierney, Anna Varakin, Mary Scholz, Nancy Magana, Liza Frye, Viviana Calderon, Gail Muhl, Michele Knorr, Sue Lysy, Chris Gallagher, Aratha Smith, and Denise Laird, who practice the lifelong enjoyment of learning we have tried to write about

- to our fellow warriors at Carroll County Public Library, including Lynn Wheeler, Tony Eckard, Ed Leiter, Nancy Haile, James Kelly, Scott Reinhart, Bob Kuntz, Muffie Smith, Ann Wisner, Lisa Back, Lauren Keppel, Ruthanne Lillis, everyone in outreach, including our wonderful volunteers, and all who loyally answered the call for help as we tried to redefine the library's purpose in motivating adults to inspire young children to learn

- to the American Library Association, the Public Library Association, the Association of Library Service to Children, and the "Every Child Ready to Read @ your library" program, for being a beacon of shining light

- to Stephanie Zvirin, and the ALA Editions staff, for their enthusiasm and savvy assistance

- most of all, to our families, whose loving support has made all the difference. Thank you, Adreon, Joe, and John, for your feedback, encouragement, patience, and humor

Introduction

This how-to book, based on public library research, is designed for anyone interested in motivating adults to increase their ability to foster school readiness and inspire children to learn. The goal to inspire all children to learn is an ambitious one. By reaching out to adults who spend time with young children and providing them sustained, high-quality training, we can greatly increase the likelihood of achieving this goal. Supplying the materials needed to implement the training adds another level of probability to the equation. Finally, making the whole process fun and engaging empowers adults to not only want to achieve school readiness for the children in their care but to feel like they can do so.

As ALA and libraries across the country learned more about brain development and early learning in the 1990s, we discovered that there was a dearth of scientific research by public libraries on the effectiveness of their early learning programs and initiatives. Dorothy Stoltz, head of outreach services and programming at Carroll County (Maryland) Public Library, became interested in conducting a study to determine the impact of library programs and services on young children. In

2004 she asked Elaine Czarnecki, a reading specialist, instructor at Johns Hopkins University, and consultant for Resources in Reading, to attend a community partnership meeting to brainstorm ideas for conducting a study. Because home child care providers were struggling to take the 54-hour course on the Maryland Model for School Readiness kindergarten assessment, a goal was established to create a brief yet focused training program with an emphasis on the language and literacy learning domain to help bridge the training gap. Connie Wilson, programming specialist, joined the team as the library's lead early literacy trainer. The subsequent training package and study showed statistically significant increases in comprehension, phonological awareness, and concepts about print in three- and four-year-olds.

Motivated by ALA's "Every Child Ready to Read @ your library" parent education initiative and Maryland libraries' "It's Never Too Early" initiative, our team created a school readiness training program designed to engage adults to be involved in a child's learning; focus on conversation, book sharing, and play; use everyday materials, books, and hands-on activities; and be fun for adults and children. This book brings that program to you.

Every Child Ready for School is divided into several parts, followed by a list of resources where you can get more information:

- **Part 1**, "Why Train Adults," describes the reasons behind the study and how the library is a cornerstone for inspiring children to learn.

- **Part 2**, "Guidelines for Training Adults," explores the proven methods for successful training of early literacy and school readiness best practices, including the importance of having a strong learning philosophy.

- **Part 3**, "Step-by-Step Guide to a Great Training Package," helps you plan and conduct the workshops, including how to encourage the use of hands-on materials and how to offer easy follow-up support. It concludes with summary points on how to invoke your ideal training yet implement a realistic training package that fits your library staffing, funding, and community.

- The afterword includes final thoughts about redefining what libraries are and what they can do.

- The appendixes offer supplemental information. Free downloadable versions of much of that information as well as posters and additional downloadable training tools can be found on the ALA Editions Web Extras page at www.alaeditions.org/webextras. References to additional online materials are included throughout the book.

Each of you will bring different backgrounds, experiences, and skills to your training. Our suggestion is this: adapt our program to what is already working for you. Although you certainly want to use these research-based strategies and do the best you can to incorporate them into your program, we encourage you to do so without making it impractical for your situation. We do believe that you will find the strategies extremely adaptable, fun, and rewarding to include in what you are already doing. Each chapter ends with a set of "Points to Ponder"—questions posed to help you think through concepts that can be insightful in creating a practical training program. It is not necessary to spend a great deal of time on the questions or to ponder every question, but please consider every point if you are inspired to do so.

This book can serve as a stand-alone manual to replicate the training from the research study, to help you create your own training, or to use with other programs such as "Every Child Ready to Read." The first six chapters give the why and how to train adults on early literacy school readiness with easy-to-do best practices for any workshop or training program. The final four chapters can be used by anyone who wants to offer something more in-depth and offers a special outline featuring our research-tested program for training child care providers.

Whether you are a librarian, teacher, child care professional, parent, or grandparent, we hope that you find useful strategies in this book so that all of us can inspire children to learn.

PART I

Why Train Adults?

CHAPTER 1

How Children Learn

Although learning is an internal process, it is the role of the adult to foster and guide children to develop a lifelong enjoyment of learning. When we as adults look at the responsibility of helping young children become ready for school not as a burden but as an opportunity to expand our own learning horizons, it creates a pleasant learning bond with the child. We are figuring out how to bring out the best in each other. We are learning together. We are having fun. Using patience, love, and everyday common sense, adults can inspire children to learn.

The important thing is not so much that every child should be taught, as that every child should be given the wish to learn.
—JOHN LUBBOCK

Brain Development

Learning begins at birth. By the end of the first day of life a baby's brain has already made thousands of connections between brain nerve cells. Brain connections grow at an extraordinary rate for the first three years and continue at a fast pace through age five. Although the brain continues to develop through the mid-twenties, the selection of the most active neural circuits takes place after age five.[1] This process reduces the weaker connections while keeping strong and well-used connections. Therefore, we want to help children develop strong connections before age five in areas that will lead to successful living, such as building a healthy social/emotional foundation.

Heredity strongly influences the number and arrangement of neurons at birth, but a child's environment is also important in determining which connections become stronger and therefore more permanent. An example of a "window of opportunity" in early learning and development is that a child's first forty-eight months are an important stage for developing emotional intelligence.[2]

Social/Emotional Development

Social/emotional development lays the foundation for all other learning. Cognitive or intellectual learning develops best if a positive emotional bond has been established with at least one important adult, such as a parent, grandparent, or child care professional. When you are interacting with babies, toddlers, and preschoolers, building a one-on-one relationship helps the child to grow and mature both socially and emotionally. Children are more responsive to guidance, role modeling, and experiences when they feel that an adult with whom they have bonded cares about them. Children need to learn to tap into and express positive emotions, such as forgiveness, empathy, and cheerfulness, and manage negative emotions, such as anxiety, anger, and guilt.[3] Everyone who interacts with young children is teaching them with every interaction. Finding teachable moments in day-to-day living is an ongoing process from birth. Healthy positive social and emotional development can be accomplished by role modeling, conversations, and intentional learning opportunities. For example, you may prepare a child for a medical shot at the doctor's office by describing the key points of the visit, discussing any feelings of fear and apprehension without false reassurance that it won't hurt, and reassuring the child that the adult will be there and it will be over quickly.

Play

Young children learn through play. Research indicates that adults can inspire babies, toddlers, and preschoolers to learn by facilitating learning through play.[4] Think how much more you retain from a workshop with fun activities and laughter as opposed to one without activities and humor. Young children learn to think by participating in pretend or dramatic play. When children are playing house or grocery store they make up their own set of rules, establish roles, and practice thinking through and acting out real-life situations. It is important to provide pretend play opportunities for a child to play with other children. Research shows that through play and emulating the adult world they observe around them, with appropriate adult guidance, children develop important lifelong skills and behaviors that can lead to successful living.[5] Examples of critical skills and behaviors that kindergarten teachers are looking for and value when children start school include:

- Displays self-regulation or self-control, that is, the ability to regulate thinking, emotions and actions—can the child sit still? follow directions?
- Plays independently and seeks out things to do

- Plays well with others
- Shares
- Cares for others; displays empathy and positive emotions and behaviors toward others
- Uses curiosity and imagination
- Perseveres; is willing to try different solutions
- Has oral language skills, including the ability to talk about experiences, ask questions, and ask for help
- Delays gratification
- Maintains optimism and motivation

These behaviors and interpersonal skills are the foundation for higher-level cognitive skills associated with reading, writing, mathematics, and science. They help children learn the dynamics of conflict resolution, problem solving, and creative thinking.

Seven Areas (or Domains) of Learning

Here is an overview of school readiness skills in the form of a list of seven areas of early learning that kindergarten teachers focus on in the classroom:[6]

- Social/emotional development—self-regulation, learns to play with others and independently, can express feelings in a healthy way
- Physical development—strengthening muscles in order to walk, run, and jump, develop fine motor skills in order to hold a crayon or pencil and tie their shoes
- Social studies—learns about community and family and the world around them, begins to grasp how things work, such as, how to fasten a button, what is a phone used for, etc.
- The arts—singing, dancing, drawing, using puppets
- Language and literacy
- Scientific thinking
- Mathematical thinking

Language and literacy, scientific thinking, and mathematical thinking involve the higher level cognitive skills. Therefore, they are areas featured most prominently in our workshops. We elaborate on them in the following sections.

Language and Literacy

Language development is an important first step in early literacy development. Singing, cooing, language play (e.g., nursery rhymes), and simply talking with children all strengthen language development. Reading books to children, retelling or making up stories with puppets, and using fingerplays (language play with coordinated hand movements) are additional age-appropriate ways to build language and make learning fun. Language development is the cornerstone of promoting school readiness. School readiness is a bridge to reading, literacy, and a lifelong enjoyment of learning.

The following is a listing of school readiness components for the language and literacy domain. The level of expectation for skill development increases as children enter the preschool years, ages three to five years.[7]

- **Understanding the alphabetic principle:** being aware that letters represent the sounds in spoken language and that this is how we read and write words.

- **Letter recognition (a subset of the alphabetic principle):** being able to recognize and name upper- and lowercase letters, usually beginning with the letters in the child's name.

- **Comprehension:** being able to listen to and understand a story that is read aloud (fiction or nonfiction) by making logical predictions, connecting the events/characters to the child's own life and experiences, answering simple questions, and understanding that stories have a beginning, middle, and end.

- **Knowledge of narrative structure:** being able to demonstrate understanding of the basic structure of stories shared at this age: main character, problem, attempts to solve the problem, solution (develops by sharing many stories in the early years).

- **Vocabulary knowledge:** having a good listening and speaking vocabulary (i.e., knowing the meanings of many words). Having a good listening vocabulary (words a child can hear and understand) and speaking vocabulary (words a child can use correctly when speaking) is important for comprehension.

- **Concepts about print:** knowing basic concepts about how print and books work, such as that print tracks from left to right and top to bottom, being able to identify the front cover and title of a book, knowing to turn the pages one at a time, and understanding that stories have a beginning, middle, and end.

- **Phonological awareness:** being aware of the sounds in spoken language, for example, rhymes and syllables. This awareness can begin with enjoying nursery rhymes together.

- **Phonemic awareness (a subset of phonological awareness):** being aware of the individual sounds, or phonemes, in spoken words (e.g., that the word *bat* has three sounds or phonemes, /b/ /a/ /t/).

- **Writing:** being able to write the letters in one's name, dictate a sentence to participate in a shared writing activity (e.g., "My favorite food is pizza!"), begin to label pictures with beginning consonants (e.g., *m* for mom).

- **Listening:** being able to attend to the speaker and gain meaning by listening, following simple directions.

- **Speaking:** being able to speak and express thoughts clearly in complete, grammatically correct sentences.

See the boxed feature for an interview with Karen Kanagy, a home child care provider who was in the treatment group of our study. Her responses demonstrate her motivation to learn and grow in order to guide and inspire her child care children to develop a lifelong enjoyment of learning.

A CHILD CARE PROVIDER SPEAKS: KAREN KANAGY

What were the strengths of the training?

The Emergent Literacy Training is one of the most beneficial trainings in which I have ever participated. Child care providers were given praise for the importance of our job in teaching young children and encouragement to expand our horizons. The training reinforced principles of child development and integrated the Maryland Model for School Readiness. Training stressed the importance of literacy awareness and the definition and explanation of the components of literacy. Child care providers were given materials and resources to use with children and to encourage parent involvement. I can't say enough about this training!

When you applied the strategies and used the kit resources, how did your children respond?

The children in my child care were most responsive to training strategies and resources. They were stimulated in many ways by becoming involved in reading and conversing about books, dramatic play, and art activities and exploring basic scientific and math principles. The children were also excited about their involvement in the Emergent Literacy Training Assessment and reading with Miss Elaine.

How did you engage the children?

I included Workshop Ready At Five box materials in the child care play area, and children were encouraged to use them as their interests developed. Books were featured during storytime, used to introduce concepts and activities, and included on our book shelves.

Which materials did you utilize?

All the materials provided by the programs were put to good use. My child care children especially liked the doctor's kit and magnetic alphabet letters. I bought several more sets of letters so we would have enough letters for everyone's name. I keep the letters in baskets close to the magnetic doors of my pantry so they're readily available for the children to use.

The kit resources provided materials related to all the domains of the Maryland Model for School Readiness. The Ready At Five cards I used with the children and also shared with parents to suggest activities they could share with their children at home. We especially loved all the books provided by the training. I strongly believe that a love of reading is one of the greatest gifts that you can give a child. My child care environment is filled with all types of books, which are readily available for children to use. Children look at or read books independently; we also share books and sometimes become involved in projects based on a specific book or author. Frequently we have a time where everyone reads their own book, including me. We love our books!

What was it that you learned that had the greatest impact?

"Play is a child's work." The training reinforced my belief in this quote and my belief that one of the most important parts of my job as a family child care provider is to enable learning for the children in my care. By providing an environment rich with materials and experiences I am giving my child care children opportunities to learn about their world, to grow as people, to expand their horizons, and to prepare themselves for life experiences.

Do you have any other insights to offer?

The library's Emergent Literacy Training motivated me to explore different avenues of literacy awareness. There are many websites that offer various resources. Some have activities to be used with children and others have informative resources. I hope to continue to grow as I explore new resources and provide my child care children with new opportunities to learn.

Scientific Thinking and Mathematical Thinking

Math and science skills require higher-level thinking and development, which begin to come together in the preschool years. You can, however, begin to develop these skills with babies and toddlers by making everyday moments meaningful through talking, playing, and interacting with your children, tapping into their curiosity and interests. Adding age-appropriate books and fun activities can empower preschool children to understand these basic concepts of science and math:

- **Number recognition and sequencing:** knows numbers, can recognize and identify them, and understands that there is order to numbers, both forward and reverse. Number recognition is a skill that is built over time with repetition.

- **One-to-one correspondence:** understands that objects can represent a number (e.g., five apples represent 5). Understanding the visual relationship between a number and objects is a key skill, especially for preschoolers.

- **Problem-solving skills:** considered to be the most complex of all intellectual functions and needed in all areas of life. It is easy to help children develop these skills because they are curious. One of the most effective ways to help preschoolers become excellent problem solvers is to engage them in conversation about problems and challenges (e.g., "How can we be fair since we have only four cookies for five people?") and finding solutions ("We'll break off a small piece from each cookie to share so that each person receives the same amount of cookie.").

· **Shapes:** recognizes and names basic shapes (e.g., rectangle, circle, triangle).

· **Sorting:** the ability to place objects in groups based on a specific rule or criterion, such as color, shape, or texture. Preschoolers become able to set their own criteria for sorting objects, such as "things that are round," "things that are made of wood."

· **Measurement:** understands the concept of using tools to determine length and height (nonstandard, i.e., paperclip chain, shoes, string; and later standard, i.e., foot-long ruler). Also understands about weight and length of objects along with such concepts as *heavier, lighter, longer,* and *shorter.* Very young children can begin to understand concepts about weight and length as you have conversations with them about everyday objects.

· **Sets:** ability to make a group of objects correspond to a given number from 1 to 10 (e.g., makes a group of four books when asked for set of 4).

· **Patterns:** a set of shapes or numbers or objects that are repeated. Children enjoy seeking out patterns in the everyday things around them.

· **Spatial concepts:** understands such concepts as *over, under, in front of, behind, beside.*

· **Scientific method:** understands activities such as asking questions, predicting, experimenting/gathering information (e.g., does an object sink or float?), observing, determining the results, and recording the results (see charting). The best way to help preschoolers begin to understand scientific method is by providing hands-on experiences and fostering curiosity about the world around them.

· **Cycles:** understands that there are repeating actions or cycles that occur consistently, such as life cycles (e.g., butterfly or frog or growth of plants). This is a higher-level concept that preschoolers can grasp over time with repetition.

· **Weather and seasons:** observe and understand the cycle of the seasons and that there are different types of weather within each season. Having children observe the outside world in their backyard or a park throughout the year and draw pictures promotes understanding of these concepts.

· **Charting:** making a graph of observations over a period of time or a picture of results from experimenting. If you plant a seed or plant with your preschooler to help learn about the growing cycle, you can also have them learn about charting and observation by having them draw pictures of different stages of the process.

- **The five senses:** see, touch, smell, hear, and taste. Using these senses to explore the world is not only developmentally appropriate but really fun.

Libraries

Parents are their child's first and best teacher. Other adults such as grandparents and child care professionals often share the role as a child's early learning teacher. What better place to make learning and fun go together than at your local public library? Librarians promote the idea that parents are their child's first and continuing teacher. Using research-based principles, librarians assist in early learning by applying their expertise in early literacy skills, children's literature, and storytime delivery. Libraries offer family-friendly spaces rich with resources such as books, music CDs, concept and school readiness kits, and educational toys or play materials. They are a meeting place for you and your children.

REASONS FOR TRAINING ADULTS TO INSPIRE CHILDREN TO LEARN

☐ A general lack of understanding exists about expectations for school readiness of children entering kindergarten. This deficit is seen across all socioeconomic groups.

☐ Research shows that success throughout the school years is directly related to children's readiness to learn entering kindergarten.

☐ The years between birth and age five support the largest critical brain growth: social, emotional, and cognitive. There is a general lack of understanding by many adults about the importance of a child's overall development during these early years.

☐ Research shows that a close, loving, supportive bond with a primary responsible adult is a keystone to a child's early development in all areas.

☐ Adults may be unaware of the importance of their role in promoting a child's healthy and successful development.

☐ Adults, even those who are nurturing, are not always knowledgeable about strategies and techniques for developing and supporting a child's successful development.

☐ Research shows that intervention programs in the early years that are backed with developmental information and based on strategies supporting healthy development are more cost effective than special programs during the school years.

☐ Have you recognized that you are more open to new ideas or trying something different when you are relaxed and having fun? List three examples.

☐ Do you strive to model a healthy restraint of negative emotions, such as anger or anxiety, in order to think clearly and act responsibly in a stressful situation? What is your best approach in doing this?

☐ What can you do to become a better problem solver? Do you focus on helping children grow in their ability and confidence to learn through trial and error?

NOTES

1. Rhoshel K. Lenroot and Jay N. Giedd, "Brain Development in Children and Adolescents: Insights from Anatomical Magnetic Resonance Imaging," *Neuroscience and Biobehavioral Reviews* 30, no. 6 (2006): 718–729.

2. "Brain Development," Zero to Three, www.zerotothree.org/child-development/braindevelopment.

3. Peter K. Smith and Craig H. Hart, eds., *Blackwell Handbook of Childhood Social Development* (Oxford: Blackwell, 2002).

4. Gwen Dewar, "The Cognitive Benefits of Play: Effects on the Learning Brain," Parenting Science, 2008, www.parentingscience.com/benefits-of-play.html.

5. Doris Bergen, "The Role of Pretend Play in Children's Cognitive Development," *Early Childhood Research and Practice* 4, no. 1 (2002), http://ecrp.uiuc.edu/v4n1/bergen.html.

6. For more on the seven learning areas domains, go to www.readyatfive.org under the category Activities. For early literacy skill information, visit www.everychildreadytoread.org and check the list of resources at the end of this book.

7. For skill development specific to infants and toddlers, see Zero to Three, www.zerotothree.org.

CHAPTER 2

Harnessing the Benefits of Collaboration

Libraries Are Natural Community Partners

Once you understand the role of responsible adults in helping children achieve school readiness, you can begin to see how the library supports this effort. Maryland's Creating Connections to Grow Readers initiative was established to encourage public libraries to use four guiding principles:

· Parents are their child's first and best teacher.

· Libraries offer parents the resources they need to foster school readiness.

· Libraries use research-based practices.

· Libraries develop community partnerships.

Creating family and community partnerships can help children enter school ready to learn. Parents may feel isolated and unsure about whether they are doing the best they can for their children. Home child care providers may also become isolated in their work and can benefit from sharing ideas and activities. Communities can pool resources to develop more and richer opportunities for families and caregivers.

The Library's Mission

Libraries are redefining what they are and what they can do. They are a vast resource for promoting a lifelong enjoyment of learning, beginning with our very

> *Coming together is a beginning. Keeping together is progress. Working together is success.*
> —HENRY FORD

youngest community members. Libraries can be a vibrant and integral part of any community if they do these things:

- Demonstrate what they can do already and what they are becoming as a portal for inspiring adults and children to enjoy lifelong learning.

- Learn to define their services by devoting themselves to meet challenges faced by communities, challenges such as children not being ready for school.

- Offer a safe, neutral, and reputable place for people of diverse backgrounds, beliefs, and experiences to come together for programs, discussion, and networking.

- Provide high-quality customer service through trained staff who can seek out and serve library patrons at their point of need or "want," including navigating, analyzing, and making recommendations of information and resources in a variety of formats, from board books to online sources.

- Offer literacy-related expertise in new and emerging technologies as well as readers' advisory.

- Offer programs and activities to meet community needs and provide opportunities for learning and enjoyment that might not otherwise be easily accessible to families geographically or financially.

- Refer library patrons to other programs and services in their community.

Libraries and Families

Libraries can motivate adults to inspire children to learn. They provide families with a door to learning for children birth to five years with a special focus on language and literacy.[1] Many libraries offer family-friendly spaces with age-appropriate books for adult/child sharing. These spaces can be created simply by providing colorful and interactive items that appeal to children, such as bright banners and puzzles, blocks, or other manipulatives, within developmentally appropriate spaces. If more resources are available, libraries can create early literacy activity centers or play-and-learn areas for children and adults to play and learn together. Language interaction, prevalent within play among children and between child and adult, is a key element to early literacy development. These areas are designed for self-directed activities. They are child-friendly, comfortable for adults, and conducive to interaction between child and adult, child and child, and adult and adult.

Libraries offer other in-library family-friendly programs and services, such as these:

- Books, music CDs, school readiness and concept kits, age-appropriate suggested reading lists along with tips on how to share books with children at different ages and other early literacy materials to borrow for home use

- Storytimes, play groups after storytimes for parents and children to have group play experiences, parent/child learning parties, and other age-appropriate programs such as literature-based puppet shows
- Workshops for adults on early literacy, school readiness, and children's literature
- Weekday, evening, and weekend hours to provide convenient times for families to learn and play together

The best bonus of all is that these library services are free.

Libraries and Child-Serving Agencies

Libraries often develop community partnerships to maximize resources and reach new audiences. Libraries strive to participate in the early childhood community's planning process, including collaborative grant writing. An early childhood coalition can include key players such as parents, child care professionals and associations, schools, Head Start, and service coordinating councils. Libraries can serve several functions in the coalition, such as offering workshops for professionals working with children on early literacy, school readiness, and children's literature. Bookmobile or other outreach services may be a way to partner with child care centers, schools, and other community programs serving children/parents, including Women, Infant, and Children (WIC) programs and other nutrition programs for parents and child care professionals.

Several years ago the Maryland Office of Children and Families created local management boards in each county to act as service coordinating councils to oversee the best local use of federal and state grant funding. Libraries promoted themselves as the perfect partners to help their communities reach the goal of every child entering school ready to succeed. A driving force for this positive change and mutual goal was the brain research of the 1990s that shows the critical window of opportunity during the first five years of a child's development.

By 2000, the Maryland State Department of Education had created the Maryland Model for School Readiness (MMSR) kindergarten assessment and instructional guidelines for achieving school readiness. Libraries and community partners began to focus their efforts on early prevention in the continuum of service starting at birth. They evaluated, changed, and expanded both individual agency programs and community collaborations. Although libraries and agencies had always worked together, using broad strategies with specific goals for early childhood development and early learning brought out the best in each. The kindergarten assessment allowed libraries and child-serving agencies to work together on facilitating school readiness.

How did Carroll County and other counties harness the power of collaboration to bring out the best in each agency? One-on-one relationships are the foundation of successful collaborations. Library, school, and community agency staff collaborated on several projects and in the process learned a great deal about how to work with each other as individuals, such as adapting to agency norms, communication, and work styles. In most cases, interagency staff members were getting to know each other for the first time. In some cases, staff knew each other personally but had never worked together. We learned the strengths and limitations of each other's organizations. Agencies learned, for example, about library staff expertise, but also about resource constraints. Of greater importance may have been the willingness of each agency representative to learn and grow as an individual to serve the greater good. This process empowered each of us to influence our organization to become more flexible in our policies and be a stronger community partner. The early childhood coalition became a winning team: for school years 2009/10 and 2010/11, Carroll County achieved the top kindergarten assessment scores in Maryland. In the 2010/11 report, 96 percent of children in home child care were fully ready for school.

Tips for Healthy Collaborations

Like many communities, ours strives to create a common knowledge base of early childhood and school readiness issues and to use a common language for talking about it. This knowledge and language are created and understood through agency-to-agency projects, such as bookmobile service to Head Start, and larger collaborative projects among several agencies, such as the "Books for Babies" project, a popular community initiative between child-serving agencies and hospitals (*see below*). Project participation creates opportunities for organizations to educate each other about their policies, limitations, and willingness to change and grow. Participation should happen at a level that works for each situation. If you have too few staff to attend community meetings, develop a set of priorities to help you focus on the most effective way to collaborate. The goal is to gain benefits without spreading you or your organization too thin. It can be done.

Setting Right Priorities

When you have to choose among several tasks, there are many ways to set the right priorities. As the saying goes, I have too much to do and too little time. If that sounds familiar, here are two guidelines to help you. Yes, we understand how challenging they might sound at first, but give them a try. They can help you focus your time and energy. In general, choose two or three top areas of focus for the year, for example, serving children birth to age five, programming for families, or reaching at-risk families through community partners. Then align your daily priorities with those two or three focus areas. Another guideline is the commonly recognized Pareto principle, which emphasizes that 20 percent of your activities will account for 80 percent of your success.[2] This principle can be an excellent reminder to concentrate on your top focus areas and to avoid straining yourself and your resources.

The rationale for some of our top priorities:

- By reaching families with children birth to age five, there is a greater potential for creating lifelong library users. Grant sources, sponsorships, and partnerships in recent years have focused on supporting services for children birth to age five, their parents, and caregivers. Longitudinal studies, such as the HighScope Perry Preschool Study, reflect the economic value of investing in public and private funding in early childhood.[3]

- By focusing on outreach, community partnerships, sponsorships, and grants we keep the library at the table in the community and take advantage of service and program opportunities and funding. Libraries can better maintain a knowledge base of their community to lead the way and to fill in the gaps of local efforts for lifelong enjoyment of learning. Libraries have a golden opportunity in each community to fulfill unmet customer needs and wants.

- By focusing on delivering resources and services using newly developed technological tools, we help position libraries for the future.

- By focusing on programming, the library becomes a destination. A tremendous benefit of staff presenting children's programming is that they establish rapport and build relationships with children, teens, parents, and other adults responsible for children.

If you do not have staff members who can attend partnership meetings, invite potential community partners to your programs. Connect with them in the library or by phone or e-mail contact. If you or your staff are able to attend a few community meetings, it can be surprising how much can be accomplished by being face-to-face, occasionally. The key is to find a way to have some regular conversation with potential community partners.

The "Books for Babies" project and the "Parents as Teachers" initiative are examples of library staff aligning library services to a community effort by attending meetings and consciously looking for opportunities to collaborate. "Books for Babies" is a popular community initiative that provides a book, early literacy and early childhood milestone information, and contact information about local resources to parents of newborns when they leave the local hospital after giving birth.[4] This project is coordinated by the library, funded through grant money from the local management board, organized into bags for distribution by student volunteers at the school, and delivered to parents of newborns by nurses at the local hospital.

The "Parents as Teachers" program is a home visitation program that mentors parents and child care professionals in early childhood development and school readiness skills specific to their individual children's needs.[5] Parent educators are trained in this nationally recognized program, which originated in St. Louis, Missouri, in 1984. Our "Parents as Teachers" program is coordinated by the Judith P. Hoyer Early Childhood Center service in the public school system (the "Judy Center"). Supported by mental health services provided by Youth Services, the program is funded through monies and in-kind contributions from the local management board and community agencies and delivered by staff from the library, school, social services, and Head Start.

An example of an agency-to-agency project is the creation of early literacy activity centers, or play-and-learn areas, in library branches. When Carroll County Public Library began to model these centers after Baltimore County Public Library centers, we were pressed for funding to develop centers in all six branches. The local management board administrator, having worked with library staff who sat on the board for several years, understood the great potential of the centers and helped the library obtain the funding to offer six complete centers.

Child care agencies can help libraries learn how to obtain state child care office approval of workshops. This approval enables child care professionals to earn credit hours that are required for their annual staff development certification when they complete workshops presented by library staff. Agencies are often willing to include library and early literacy information in their newsletters. They can promote library services for professionals and parents—for example, workshops, bookmobile service, and other resources available through the library. These agencies and associations can also include library trainings in their scheduled opportunities for parents and professionals.

These priorities—building relationships, creating common knowledge, and serving on boards and committees—may seem time consuming at first, but the long-term reward is that the library is recognized as an important asset in creating a high-performing community team and is a stakeholder in helping to meet community needs. We benefit by having good communication with each other and with public officials, funders, and other key stakeholders.

Librarians, parents, home child care providers, and teachers can find many avenues to develop long-lasting relationships, join successful collaborations with other allies in early childhood development, and share in the results of stronger families and communities. See the Tips for Healthy Community Collaboration sidebar for ideas from Sari Felman and Barbara Jordan.[6]

☐ Do you take a few extra minutes when having a conversation with community partners to chat about what is important to them personally—family? travel?—to look for connections beyond the workplace? If you already have a personal relationship with a community partner, how can you elevate the professional relationship?

☐ Can you see the value of being someone who reaches out to help a partner (within the scope of your organization's resources) solve a problem, regardless of how the problem was created?

☐ When working with community partners, do you understand the importance of balancing how to give them time and space to fulfill their priorities with how to be proactive using gentle persistence to encourage them to honor their commitments?

TIPS FOR HEALTHY COMMUNITY COLLABORATION

☐ Build on existing relationships.

☐ Learn about each other's services and share resources.

☐ Join existing coalitions and networks.

☐ Meet with leaders individually and in small groups in informal settings.

☐ Invite partners to your internal meetings from time to time.

☐ Hold joint trainings and cross-train each other's staff.

☐ Market each other's services.

☐ Use written agreements as appropriate to help minimize miscommunication and create positive expectations.

☐ Be proactive in group problem solving that allows all partners to benefit.

☐ Write collaborative grants and initiate new programs and services in partnership, even if only to reach a wider audience.

☐ Be open and expect change.

☐ Help each other succeed.

NOTES

1. Kathleen Reif, "Are Public Libraries the Preschooler's Door to Learning?" *Public Libraries* 39, no. 5 (2000): 262–265.

2. For one explanation, see "Pareto Principle: How the 80/20 Rule Helps Us Be More Effective," Pinnicle Management, www.pinnicle.com/Articles/Pareto_Principle/pareto_principle.html.

3. See "HighScope Perry Preschool Study," HighScope, www.highscope.org/content.asp?contentid=219.

4. For the "Books for Babies" project, see www.ala.org/altaff/products_services/booksforbabies.

5. For "Parents as Teachers," see www.parentsasteachers.org.

6. Sari Felman and Barbara Jordan, "Together Is Better: The Role of Libraries as Natural Community Partners," *Zero to Three* 21, no. 3 (2001): 30–37.

Carroll County's Early Literacy and School Readiness Training Assessment Project

Carroll County Public Library's community partnership resulted in raising the awareness of the importance and need for high-quality adult interaction with young children to achieve school readiness. In Carroll County, a specific need was identified for professional child care programs.

Several longitudinal studies suggest dramatic outcomes for children who participate in high-quality early childhood programs. Children who are ready to succeed when they enter kindergarten make and sustain good grades throughout their school career; are 50 percent less likely to be involved in crime; and are more likely to graduate from high school, get a job, make more money, and get married and start a family.

Spearheaded by Art Rolnick, the Federal Reserve Bank of Minneapolis, in collaboration with the University of Minnesota, has been a leader in reviewing and sponsoring studies that assess the costs and returns of early childhood programs.[1] Some studies indicate a significant economic benefit from investing in early childhood development. For example, the HighScope Perry Preschool Study followed 123 children through age forty. It showed a rate of return of 16 percent related to the above list of outcomes. In economic terms, that means $16 saved in the teen and adult years for each dollar invested in a high-quality early childhood

> *Don't judge each day by the harvest you reap, but by the seeds you plant.*
> —ROBERT LOUIS STEVENSON

program. Other studies show cost-benefit ratios ranging from a $4–$7 return for each dollar investment.

Two National Research Council reports—*From Neurons to Neighborhoods: The Science of Early Childhood Development* (2000) and *Eager to Learn: Educating Our Preschoolers* (2001)—helped libraries and community partners understand brain development research, the importance of social and emotional development as a foundation for all other learning, and how to set standards for early learning.[2] Libraries focused on developing programs and services to reaffirm their role in helping children become ready for school and to strengthen partnerships with parents and caregivers.[3]

Background to Library Research

Public libraries have been striving to promote research-based early literacy development since the onset of the Public Library Association's (PLA) Early Literacy Project in 2000, when a partnership was formed with the National Institute of Child Health and Human Development. This partnership resulted in the successful "Every Child Ready to Read" initiative with PLA and the Association of Library Services to Children.[4] Since 1998, Maryland public libraries have been striving to meet the same goals as the "Every Child Ready to Read" initiative, with their "It's Never Too Early" campaign.

In 1998, Harriet Henderson, along with Kathleen Reif, director of the Wicomico Public Library, and Stephanie Shauck, a youth services consultant for the Maryland State Department of Education, decided that libraries should spread the word about the importance of language development and early literacy skills to a broader audience.[5] They, along with Gail Griffith from Carroll County, Micki Freeny from Prince George's County, Lynne Lockwood from Baltimore County, Ellen Riordan of Enoch Pratt Library, and other Maryland library administrators, mentored library staff. Three main areas of focus were brain development and early learning, the economic value of reaching children birth to age five, and the importance of being at the table with public officials and community partners.

Several Maryland librarians became involved at the national and state levels— Saroj Ghoting, Betsy Diamant-Cohen, Kathleen MacMillan, Dorothy Stoltz, Connie Wilson, and others. They were inspired by their mentors and by "Every Child Ready to Read" to help reinvent the role of public libraries in early learning. In 2001/2, the Maryland State Department of Education, Division of Library Development and Services, used Institute for Museum and Library Services (IMLS) Library Services Technology Act funds to arrange for reading specialists from Johns Hopkins University, Elaine Czarnecki and Gilda Martinez, to present a statewide series of workshops for Maryland librarians, promoting the use of research-based early literacy best practices in storytimes and outreach to parents and caregivers.[6]

The workshop series also helped librarians begin sharing school readiness tips with adults during library storytimes. These readiness tips explained in a sentence or two the knowledge or skills being developed by specific actions during stories or activities and encouraged the adults to do the same at home as their child's "first teacher." As an example, one of the tips was "By encouraging your child to talk about his favorite part of a storybook, you are helping him develop his narrative skills and build vocabulary." After this statewide initiative, we formed a team in 2004 to design a research study, again funded by the IMLS to the Division of Library Development and Services. This study—the Early Literacy Training Assessment Project—involved home child care providers and the three- and four-year-olds in their care.

Early Literacy Training Assessment Project

Although Carroll County (population 167,000) is predominantly a white, middle-class community in a rural/suburban setting, there are pockets of poverty throughout the area. The county has top-performing schools and a library with one of the state's highest per capita circulations. In 2003/4 many children in the county entering school scored below the state average on the kindergarten assessment. Fifty-three percent were not ready in the language and literacy learning domain. It became a priority for the library to help parents and child care professionals increase their understanding of school readiness beyond what was being offered. Although the library had developed and presented early literacy training workshops, we saw a critical need to develop specific training to address our community's kindergarten expectations and to assess the effectiveness of that training.

Other states may not have a kindergarten assessment and instructional system such as the MMSR. Nevertheless, its seven learning areas or domains offer a common understanding, a common language, and a set of goals that help parents, child care professionals, librarians, teachers, and others support children's learning from birth. These learning domains are universal to all communities and are research-based. As described in chapter 1, they include social/emotional development, physical development and health, language and literacy, mathematical thinking, scientific thinking, social studies, and the arts.

The library turned to child care professionals, specifically home child care providers, for the research study for several reasons. First, many child care providers spend more hours with children than do the parents. Second, it was easier to conduct a study using a group of child care professionals than parents—each provider impacts more children than a single family and providers actively seek out training opportunities. Third, many providers are enthusiastic learners because they tend to be isolated in their business and welcome an opportunity to exchange ideas. Fourth, providers often have a low adult-child ratio, which gives them a unique opportunity to create a trusting bond over several years with children in their care. Fifth, a gap in training existed in 2004 for home child care providers related to the MMSR kindergarten assessment, with only 2 percent of providers completing the 54-hour training course offered by the Department of Education. This training gap motivated us to revamp the library's early literacy training and offer a brief yet focused training package. The goal—to determine whether the library's training made an impact on the early literacy skills of three- and four-year-olds—became the cornerstone for our research project. We named the project Early Literacy Training Assessment Project (ELTAP). The research assessment concluded that the ELTAP model resulted in improved understanding and implementation of best practices in early literacy by home child care providers, which then resulted in growth in the children's early literacy skills.

ELTAP enhances the "Every Child Ready to Read" model primarily in two ways: it specifically incorporates Maryland's requirements for school readiness to better align with local school and community needs, and it expands the training to include additional components consistent with effective professional development, namely hands-on materials and continued support beyond the initial training.

The target group was home child care providers in communities where a significant number of Carroll County students had been assessed as "not ready" in the area of language and literacy when they entered kindergarten. Library partners in the project included Susan Mitchell, intervention services coordinator and director of the school district's Judith P. Hoyer Early Child Care and Education Enhancement Program, which serves low-income children from birth to five years old; Kris Holocker, of the Carroll County Child Care Referral and Resource Center; Denise Magee and Barb Summers, of the Carroll County Home Child Care Association, and Elaine Czarnecki, a reading consultant.

A true experimental research design was used for the study; random selection, by ORC MACRO, a research design firm, was used to assign the providers who volunteered to either a treatment group (received the training) or a control group (did not receive the training). Forty home child care providers were identified to participate in the study. The majority of the providers resided in Title I school districts, and all had three- and four-year-olds, our target ages, in their care.

The assessment consisted of two main components: pre- and post-surveys (before and after the training program), vetted by ORC MACRO, of child care providers on their knowledge of early literacy development and the activities/materials they used to foster this development in their child care setting; and pre- and post-assessment of the three- and four-year-olds in their care on the key areas of early literacy.

Two assessment visits were made to each provider in the treatment group, one in the fall and one in the spring. A survey tool was mailed to each provider. We then visited each provider's home, chatted with them about the project, answered questions and collected the surveys, met the children, and assessed them individually. The assessment tool chosen for the children, the Early Literacy Skills

Assessment (ELSA), was developed by the HighScope Educational Research Foundation. This assessment was particularly well suited to the study, since it assessed the children in the areas of story comprehension, phonological awareness, the alphabetic principle, and concepts about print, which would all be focus areas of the upcoming early literacy training for the providers. In addition, the ELSA provided an authentic assessment experience for the three- and four-year-olds, in that the questions are embedded in a storybook that is read aloud to a child in a one-on-one setting.[7]

Fall visit: ELSA administration

In the spring, we repeated the same sequence for the post-assessment. We mailed surveys, visited the providers in both groups, collected the surveys, and assessed the children with the ELSA. We scored the assessments and mailed reports to both providers and parents. Resources in Reading then submitted the data to ORC MACRO to run a statistical analysis on the raw data.

The Training Model

The ELTAP team next focused its energy on creating a total training package that would motivate home child care providers. The training consisted of three components (*elaborated in chapters 7–10*):

Workshops: fall and spring workshops (4.5 total hours) based on the MMSR in all domains or areas of learning but focused on language and literacy

Hands-on activities and materials: early literacy materials and activities for the providers to use in their child care homes to help implement the training—books, puppets, magnetic letters, CDs of children's songs

Support: newsletters to help the providers implement the training with their new materials as well as phone conversations to give them the opportunity to discuss the new activities they were trying, ask questions, and share problems

Workshops

The workshops were conducted in fall 2005 and spring 2006. The fall three-hour workshop was planned and delivered to provide hands-on training in the research-based components of early literacy. At this event, providers received an extensive kit of materials to use in their child care homes to support the early literacy concepts and techniques shared during the training. This kit, consisting of interactive materials such as toys for pretend play, picture books, and magnetic letters, was compiled from a variety of early childhood resources. The kit also included Ready At Five School Readiness Activity Cards, produced by the Ready At Five Partnership (www.readyatfive.org), a part of the Maryland Business Roundtable dedicated to helping children start school ready to learn (*see appendix A*).

Describing the take-home materials during the fall workshop.

Each provider was also given a binder of written support materials with information on brain development research plus additional activities, songs, fingerplays, and book lists. Participants were familiarized with the information in the binder as each area was covered in the workshop: brain research and its relationship to early childhood development, the importance of pretend play, positive social/emotional development based on research, and the importance of the provider's relationship with the children as a role model and teacher. We modeled extensively and provided practice opportunities throughout the workshop to help ensure that active learning was taking place, and we emphasized that most learning occurs in a relaxed, secure environment. Shared fun, rather than drill or rote memory exercise, is the ideal method.

We also reviewed exactly what skills and abilities kindergarten teachers are looking for when they assess how prepared their students are for school when they arrive in the fall. (Note: Although the Common Core State Standards were not in place at the time of our study, sharing these in the workshop would be an example of connecting to school readiness expectations.) The child care providers participated in an exercise designed to assist them in understanding

Child care professionals discussing how to enhance learning by doing activities related to a picture book.

the criteria Maryland kindergarten teachers use when assessing a child in language and literacy. Many providers commented on how this helped them explain early literacy concepts to parents. The enthusiasm was high as providers left the training with all of their new materials, ready to apply what they had learned.

The spring workshop was designed to give the providers an opportunity to share the activities that had worked well for them and others they had developed on their own to have fun with the children while promoting school readiness skills. Additional training during this second workshop also included use of a reading ring of questions and tips developed to help them use techniques for building comprehension. We also included informal assessment tools, called "Snapshots," to evaluate ongoing skill development in the four areas of early literacy development. Time was dedicated during the training to encouraging and helping providers brainstorm and share ideas with each other for involving the parents in reinforcing the learning taking place in the child care setting.

Additional materials to reinforce phonological awareness skills, such as rhyming and beginning sound card sets, were distributed as well. Providers were enthusiastic about sharing what they had accomplished with the children in their care.

Support

Two newsletters were created to refine and extend providers' knowledge of best practices in the components of early literacy development from the training: oral language and comprehension, phonological awareness, the alphabetic principle, and concepts about print. The newsletters were mailed to the treatment group

Spring training

providers in December 2005 and in the winter of 2006. Each mailing included additional literacy materials, in the form of puppets and music CDs, for use in their child care homes.

Telephone contact was made with the providers in the treatment group twice during the project, within six weeks after the fall workshop and once again six weeks prior to the follow-up workshop, to discuss their progress with the new techniques and materials as well as answer any questions. A sampling of their comments was included in the winter newsletter so they could share ideas and encourage each other. The following examples provide a snapshot of their enthusiasm for the new activities they were trying:

> The children love the puppets. Besides reading storybooks, I use puppets to tell little made-up stories. The children now ask, "Will you tell me a story from your head?"

> Having new things to use from the activity kit is motivating the children and motivating me, too.

Benefits for the Children

The results of the assessment indicated that the treatment had a positive effect on both the children's performance and the providers' knowledge of early literacy. Figure 3.1 illustrates the comparison of raw score gains from both groups in the four test areas. Because there were different numbers of children in the treatment and control groups, we looked at the data by comparison of percentages of children in each group. As this bar graph indicates, the greatest difference was in the area of comprehension, where more than 50 percent of the children in the treatment group increased their scores by six or more points, as compared to none of the children in the control group. The areas of phonological awareness and concepts about print had significant gains in raw score points for the treatment group, and the alphabetic principle area had a slight gain in raw score points for the treatment group.

FIG. 3.1 *Percentage of Children Whose Raw Score Increased By 6 or More Points*

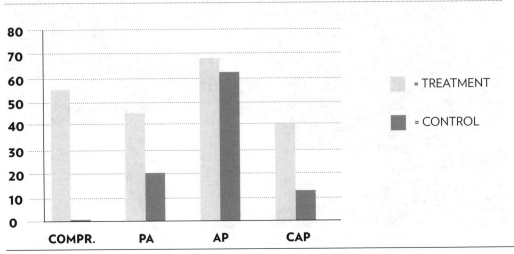

To complete a statistical analysis of the ELSA results, regression analysis was used to isolate the treatment effect in each of the four test areas individually. The final test results showed the treatment effect to be statistically significant in three of the four areas: comprehension, phonological awareness, and concepts about print. In the area of the alphabetic principle, although the children in the treatment group did show more of a gain than the children in the control group, it was not a wide enough margin to be considered statistically significant.

Table 3.1 llustrates the main findings from the regression analysis. The first column lists the four test areas. The second column shows the treatment effect (the results of attending the workshops, using play materials, and responding to support) in raw score points for each test area. For example, a child who received the treatment (his or her provider received the training package) would be expected to score approximately six points higher in comprehension than a child who had not received the treatment. The third column shows whether the treatment effect in this area was found to be statistically significant, and the last column shows the level of statistical significance, or p-value. The treatment effect for comprehension was significant at the .001 level, or very highly significant; the probability of this gain being attributed to chance is 1 in 1,000.

TABLE 3.1 *Regression Analysis*

Treatment area	Treatment effect	Treatment effect significant?	Significance level
Comprehension	6.479	Yes	<.001
Phonological awareness	2.137	Yes	<.05
Alphabetic principle	3.263	No	>.05
Concepts about print	3.269	Yes	<.001

The pre- and post-survey of child care providers included both selected response questions and opportunities for open-ended response. It was designed to assess changes in understanding and application of key early literacy concepts. The final survey results showed a statistically significant change for the treatment group versus the control group on the majority of the questions.

As a final survey question for the treatment group, providers were asked to indicate how helpful the professional development resources (workshops, materials, and support) had been to them and to provide examples of how these resources had affected their early literacy programs. One hundred percent of the providers indicated that the resources had been "very helpful."

The following is a sampling of their responses to the open-ended follow-up question on the survey:

They have definitely rejuvenated me with ideas and excitement! Newsletters have continued to reinforce ways we can teach reading in day-to-day activities. Music is now a daily activity due to great resources.

Newsletters are awesome, it is nice to see other ideas that other providers have and use them. The books we've read and activities we've done, letters on the fridge, children also traced them to learn, the bean bags—we played games with, the dishes—all was used.

The suggested books and music CDs in the newsletters were great. It was nice especially with the books—they were excellent choices that all the children loved!

Conclusions

The training had significant effects on both the children's performance and the providers' knowledge of how to promote early literacy development in their child care homes. Promoting oral language development through the children's active participation in storybook read-alouds, pretend play, and "hands-on" learning experiences was a major component of the workshops and newsletters. Inasmuch as the answers to comprehension questions on the ELSA are scored for relevance and complexity of ideas expressed, it was not surprising that the area of highest gain was in comprehension. This finding was particularly significant due to the fact that in the pre- and post-surveys providers in both the treatment and control groups reported reading to the children at least once a day. This suggests that participation in the treatment group produced a change in the quality of the read-aloud experience—that is, more verbal interaction between the child and the adult, in the form of actively engaging the child to participate by asking questions, making predictions, discussing interesting vocabulary and story events, and so forth.

Neuman and Celano reported a similar finding from their two-year program to put high-quality children's books in urban child care centers. Adults were also provided with training on how to help children get more from the books they shared with them. Findings from this study suggest that "it is not just exposure to books that makes a difference." In addition, "children need skillfully mediated assistance that can help to explain the workings of literacy . . . It is the intensity of engagement, the quality of talk and conversational interactions between adult and child, that nurtures and helps them to construct vital literacy-related concepts."[8]

The importance of the *unconstrained* skills of vocabulary, comprehension, and background knowledge to children's long-term success in reading and the content areas is emphasized in the second edition of *Every Child Ready to Read @ your library*.[9] Unconstrained skills are skills that have the potential to continue to develop over one's lifetime, as opposed to constrained skills, such as letter knowledge and phonological awareness, which have a finite end to their development (e.g., once a child learns the letters of the alphabet, that skill development is complete). Though both sets of skills are important to reading development, developing vocabulary, comprehension, and background knowledge in the early years are critical to later success.

An examination of the providers' responses to the open-ended survey questions reveals a deeper understanding of the key early literacy principles for those participating in the treatment group, as evidenced by the complexity of their responses. An understanding of the importance of active learning for the young children in their care was also evident. Of final note is the enthusiasm expressed by the providers in the treatment group for the professional development they had received. Community partners shared with us that this experience had motivated their child care providers more than any other training experience in recent years.

Spring visit: The children were excited to show what they had learned.

Implications for Public Libraries

ELTAP contributes to the research base in early literacy and collaborative efforts among libraries, communities, and schools. In their chapter "Preparation of Early Childhood Professionals," the authors of *Eager to Learn: Educating Our Preschoolers* cite the importance of adult training related to positive outcomes for children.[10] Our treatment resulted in improved understanding and implementation of best practices in early literacy by family child care providers, which then resulted in growth in the children's early literacy skills. We believe this is promising news for public libraries that may see a similar need in their communities and wish to build upon the "Every Child Ready to Read" goals in a training package specific to their state or local school kindergarten standards.

What caused this level and intensity of intervention to produce such positive effects in the time span of one school year? Part of the explanation may be that, compared to other training opportunities, the treatment in this study included both professional development training and the materials needed to support the use of best practices in child care homes. Modeling and guided practice combined with actually being able to take the materials back to use with the children may have contributed to the success of the treatment. The activities were content rich and developmentally appropriate. To quote Susan B. Neuman, former U.S. Assistant Secretary of Education, "Low-income preschool children need content rich instruction, not drill in procedural skills."[11] Another contributing factor may have been the ongoing contact in the form of detailed newsletters, additional resources, and phone conversations that provided sustained support for implementing the training concepts. The providers were empowered to feel they could truly make a difference for the children in their care.

The successful project was extended for a second year in 2006/7 in order to provide additional details in the evaluation of the effectiveness of the training program, document the progression of literacy competency over time, and validate the findings from the first study. Based on the first year's feedback from participants and debriefing of the trainers, we increased the length of the first workshop to four hours and the second workshop to two hours.

Our most significant finding based on year two of the study was that the original treatment, or training package, had a similar effect on the early literacy

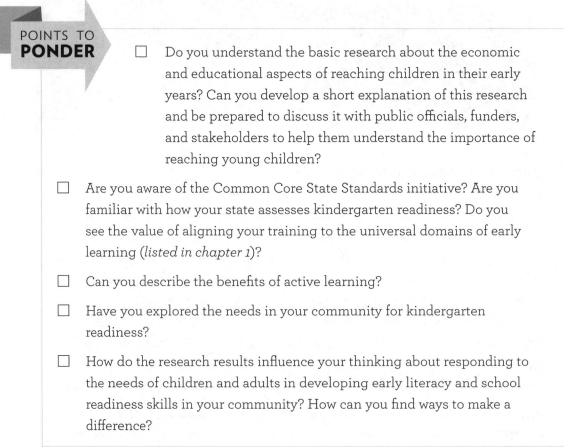

POINTS TO PONDER

☐ Do you understand the basic research about the economic and educational aspects of reaching children in their early years? Can you develop a short explanation of this research and be prepared to discuss it with public officials, funders, and stakeholders to help them understand the importance of reaching young children?

☐ Are you aware of the Common Core State Standards initiative? Are you familiar with how your state assesses kindergarten readiness? Do you see the value of aligning your training to the universal domains of early learning (*listed in chapter 1*)?

☐ Can you describe the benefits of active learning?

☐ Have you explored the needs in your community for kindergarten readiness?

☐ How do the research results influence your thinking about responding to the needs of children and adults in developing early literacy and school readiness skills in your community? How can you find ways to make a difference?

development of the children and the early literacy knowledge base of the providers with the new group. The results confirmed our conclusions from year one. By providing the treatment for the original control group, we were able to once again examine the effects of the training package, by determining their growth from the pretest of the ELSA to the posttest, and by comparing their performance to the performance of the children who received the treatment the first year. In addition, the fact that the four-year-olds in the original treatment group performed well in year two shows that they maintained their early literacy skills.

Findings suggest that the difference between receiving training and support and not receiving training and support is so large that the gain from some additional training for a second year is relatively small. These findings have guided us to consider our staffing limitations and first focus our efforts on reaching as many adults as possible with the training package, as opposed to offering a second training package. This is just one example of how to apply the study findings to your own particular situation.

NOTES

1. For access to the studies, see "Special Studies: Early Childhood Development," Federal Reserve Bank of Minneapolis, www.minneapolisfed.org/publications_papers/studies/earlychild/.

2. Jack P. Shonkoff and Deborah A. Phillips, eds., *From Neurons to Neighborhoods: The Science of Early Childhood Development* (Washington, DC: National Academies Press, 2000); Suzanne Donovan and M. Susan Burns, *Eager to Learn: Educating Our Preschoolers* (Washington, DC: National Academies Press, 2001).

3. "Research Studies and Task Force Reports Can Help You Advocate for High-Quality Early Childhood Education," National Association for the Education of Young Children, www.naeyc.org/files/naeyc/ResearchStudies.pdf.

4. *Every Child Ready to Read @ your library*, 2nd ed., www.everychildreadytoread.org.

5. Walter Minkel, "It's Never Too Early," *School Library Journal* 48, no. 7 (2002): 38–42, available at www.schoollibraryjournal.com/article/CA225245.html.

6. Gilda Martinez, "Libraries, Families, and Schools: Partnership to Achieve School Reading Readiness; A Multiple Case Study of Maryland Public Librarians," *Children and Libraries* 5, no. 1 (2007): 32–39.

7. "Early Literacy Skills Assessment (ELSA)," HighScope, www.highscope.org/file/BookPages/ELSAFullPresentationDocument0105.pdf.

8. Susan B. Neuman and Donna Celano, "Books Aloud: A Campaign to Put Books in Children's Hands," *Reading Teacher* 54, no. 6 (March 2001): 550–557.

9. *Every Child Ready to Read @ your library*, 2nd ed., www.everychildreadytoread.org/project-history%09/literature-review-2010.

10. Donovan and Burns, *Eager to Learn*, 261–276.

11. Susan B. Neuman, "N Is for Nonsensical," *Educational Leadership*, October 2006, 28–31.

PART II

Guidelines for Training Adults

CHAPTER 4

Intentional Training

In this chapter we share our study's guidelines for developing training for adults. You may find them helpful for your own training program. One of the guidelines is based on the Carroll County Public Library model of an organizational learning philosophy with two guiding principles. The term *learning philosophy* may seem a little overwhelming or off-putting in the context of promoting school readiness. You may ask why we care about a learning philosophy when presenting to adults. We care because your learning philosophy reflects your goals and attitudes about the learning process and how you instill them in your workshop participants for more proactive and long-lasting results.

I am always ready to learn, although I do not always like being taught.
—WINSTON CHURCHILL

The first guiding principle is that we each are responsible for our own learning. It is an underlying tenet of this book and of our training program. We want to pass along this principle to all those who train, teach, and mentor others who foster school readiness in young children. Bring out your best as a trainer by being a master learner. The second principle is that learning is reinforced when you teach others something that you have learned. The best way to learn something is by seeing or hearing about a concept, doing or practicing it, and finally teaching the concept to someone else. Parents and child care providers can learn more in the training program when they share and discuss their observations of their children's learning and the success or failure of a specific activity.

The First Principle: You Are Responsible for Your Own Learning

Beginning a training workshop by establishing the mindset that we are each responsible for our own learning is a powerful asset for effective training. It fosters an open, collaborative environment that helps participants ask and answer questions, reflect on their practices in their own settings, and see how the content of the workshop could affect those practices.

What does it mean to have the learning philosophy that you are responsible for your own learning in a training session? It means that *during the training session,* you are an active, responsive, and respectful participant; you embrace the possibilities of new ideas; and you think about ways to apply (and perhaps adapt) the information being shared to your own particular setting, the population you serve, and your resources. To foster these principles actively, it is imperative that time be taken at the beginning of a training workshop to elaborate the importance of this mindset to the workshop's success.

As the trainer, you can list the learning philosophy principles in an abbreviated manner. Emphasize that you respect the participants' interest in learning by their giving up time to help the children in their care. Strongly encourage them to take advantage of ways to reinforce their own learning during the workshops. For example, point out the availability of sticky notes and notepads to make notes. Emphasize that this is an opportunity to share ideas, knowledge, skills, experiences, and information—including using the larger group for further discussion and problem solving about how their children may respond to an activity. In our trainings, adults have said that these opportunities for reflection and discussion are some of the most appreciated aspects of the training. For example, you might hear people asking questions or sharing how an activity could work in their setting, and you see them taking notes or participating in a group activity. A brief opening such as this sets the tone for an engaging workshop and helps all participants see how important they are to the success of the training session.

What does it mean to have the learning philosophy that you are responsible for your own learning after the workshop? It means that, *after the training session,* you take advantage of formal and informal learning opportunities; seek challenging and intellectual stimulation; take reasonable risks to try something new; venture into the realm of curiosity; and reinforce your own learning by sharing information with others, such as parents and peers.

As the trainer, encourage participants to adapt a broad view of learning for themselves and for the children in their care. Learning activities can occur anywhere and under any circumstance to increase knowledge, enhance a skill, and adapt to change. Each person can strive to become a lifelong learner by consistently evaluating what worked well and what could have been done differently in a situation to produce better results. See the boxed feature for an interview with Erin Mullinix, a home child care provider who was in the treatment group of our study. Her responses capture the essence of what we mean by intentional training with the underlying learning philosophy that you are responsible for your own learning.

A CHILD CARE PROVIDER SPEAKS: ERIN MULLINIX

What do you think is effective about this training?

Many trainers, while good intentioned, only tell you what to do—and then you are on your own to carry the ideas and activities through. This training gave us the tools and supplies needed to be successful with an extra opportunity to bring back and share with peers and the trainers the results from working with the children. Specifically, the resource binder was exceptionally helpful. As child care providers who work alone, the accessibility of this resource helped us to start applying the strategies and utilizing the activities right away.

What did you take away with you that you could use?

I personally felt confident about my role in encouraging learners at an early age. I realized our interactions make a huge impact on their kindergarten readiness as well as their lifelong enjoyment of reading. I began to gain respect and acknowledgment from the parents in my program about my role as an educator through their involvement.

How has the training changed the way you interact with children?

I ask more open-ended questions and really take my time with stories. I do picture walks, more predicting, reread, and have the children retell the stories. I am more intentional with the activities around the book. I also help the children learn more about the authors and illustrators.

Can you give some examples of how the strategies impacted the children?

The children were given knowledge and skills in a fun and positive way which helped them develop a lifelong love of reading. The use of all the tools and opportunities such as fingerplays, songs, role play, and puppets helped them to develop into successful readers. They are more observant of the titles, the pictures, the words, the author, and the illustrator.

What recommendations do you have for other child care professionals?

You do not need to spend a fortune to bring literacy to life for children. My experiences with the trainers and my peers brought that to light. There are many "tools" right at our fingertips, and we just have to know how to use them.

The Second Principle: The Power of the "See It, Do It, Teach It" Approach

Have you ever had the experience of learning something new, trying it for yourself, and then sharing your excitement (and perhaps frustration) with others who were also acquiring this same new skill? Reinforced learning is a powerful tool, but one that requires more than a one-shot workshop with participants. Providing opportunities for people to come back together in a follow-up workshop, to share what went well and what didn't quite go as planned when new skills were applied, extends learning and fosters true ownership of best practices. As adults learn from one other, they are empowered and motivated to continue growing and problem solving together. Thinking in advance about ways to make this continued connection is worth the effort when you are planning training opportunities. Opportunities for continued contact between participants and trainers may include newsletters that share additional tips and comments from workshop participants about the new skills/techniques; online blogs or discussion boards (see appendix B); phone conversations; and follow-up workshops to share and celebrate what is working, provide new information, and discuss how to refine and extend application of skills and techniques.

An opportunity for continued contact and learning among participants after the training is a strategy called *peer coaching,* in which two or more adults use self-reflection, constructive feedback, and discussion with each other. Statistical support for peer coaching can be found in the following data.[1]

- Five percent of learners transfer a new skill into their practice as a result of theory.
- Ten percent transfer a new skill into their practice with theory and demonstration.
- Twenty percent transfer a new skill into their practice with theory and demonstration and practice within the training.
- Twenty-five percent transfer a new skill into their practice with theory and demonstration, practice within the training, and feedback.
- Ninety percent transfer a new skill into their practice with theory and demonstration, practice within the training, feedback, and coaching.

Peer coaching puts into action the principle "see it, do it, teach it." You can encourage your participants to partner with one or more of their peers from the workshop to become mentors and support each other. Encourage participants to reflect individually on what they are doing and what the results are, and to do this in their setting. Ideally partners will observe each other, reflect on their performance, and talk about it with each other using friendly, supportive language and feedback. For many, especially home child care providers, direct observation may be difficult; they may find using regular phone contact or getting together to talk about their experiences and the children's responses a more convenient approach. This can be helpful for learning, especially after they try an activity for the first time, adapt a technique, or introduce a new storybook to their program. Questions may include what worked about this technique or activity or storybook and what could have been done differently. Encouraging adults to observe and coach each other in a friendly supportive environment is another powerful way to extend learning.

TIPS FOR PEER COACHING

Ask yourself questions such as

☐ What worked?

☐ What could I have done differently?

Three to six times a year, meet with or telephone a colleague/friend to talk about your experience and the children's responses after you conduct an activity, adapt a technique, or use a new storybook with your children.

POINTS TO PONDER

☐ Do you set aside time for self-reflection in order to enhance your own learning opportunities?

☐ Do you ask yourself questions such as what worked well, or what should I continue doing, to produce similar results next time? Do you ask yourself questions such as what could I have done differently, to produce better results next time?

☐ Have you articulated a learning philosophy and applied this philosophy to your training opportunities? Specifically, what would you do to apply a learning philosophy to your workshop?

☐ Do you see the value of moving beyond one-shot workshops to a structure of continued opportunities for participants to learn and grow together? What kind of continued opportunities would you implement in your training package?

NOTE

1. Jean M. Becker, "Peer Coaching for Improvement of Teaching and Learning," Teachers Network Leadership Institute, http://teachersnetwork.org/TNLI/research/growth/becker.htm.

CHAPTER 5

Training with a Light Touch

In this chapter we look at some simple training techniques for engaging, energizing, and building rapport with your participants. These can help you identify methods for creating a successful learning environment and an effective presentation for the adult learner, developing a skill set aimed specifically for training adults to foster school readiness.

> *Learning is a treasure that will follow its owner everywhere.*
> —CHINESE PROVERB

You can build good rapport with your audience by knowing your material, presenting clearly and simply, and using humor and conviction. A strong beginning demonstrating enthusiasm, appreciation, and respect for the participants sets the right tone and welcoming atmosphere for the training. In school readiness trainings, you want participants to think in a different way, that is, to think from a child's point of view. Children are naturally inquisitive. Encourage your audience to anticipate questions that children might ask and how they might answer those questions. Note, though, that the goal is to ask participants to become *childlike* in their engagement, not *childish*.

Create active learning opportunities in the training by using hands-on and experimental activities. You can increase the learning success rate by following some simple guidelines:

- Use a one-on-one conversation style by looking at one person at a time for each thought or sentence.

- Strive to connect with everyone in the training.

- Put your best voice forward.

- Don't take yourself too seriously.

- Start and finish on time.

- Don't overuse "I."

Make Learning a Pleasure, Not a Chore

The best workshops are those that involve humor, include modeling and guided practice, and provide opportunities for sharing and reflection among the participants. Because you want your workshop participants to come away from the training thinking "I'm ready to try this!" it is particularly important to provide modeling of the best practices you are attempting to impart. But modeling alone is not enough if you expect people really to use these new techniques. Participants must have the opportunity to "try out" the techniques in a supportive setting to help ensure transfer of learning to the home or workplace. Fortunately, all of this interaction creates a fun and engaging workshop.

An important consideration in planning and conducting workshops for adults who work with young children is transferring the message that, just as a fun, engaging workshop left them feeling informed and energized, this same premise applies to planning learning activities for the children in their care. During the workshop emphasize that learning for young children should not be formal or use rote activities as in elementary school. Make learning fun, engage the children, model what you want them to be able to do, and give them many opportunities to practice in a supportive setting. This is the approach you see promoted in our training package.

Applying the Model to Early Literacy Training

Here are five basic steps to follow:

1. **Start with an early literacy concept.** *Example:* The importance of language development to comprehension.

2. **Decide on background/content knowledge to develop with participants.** *Example:* Research shows that children who enter school with a strong listening and speaking vocabulary have a head start when learning to read.[1] One of the best ways to build children's vocabulary is to have frequent conversations with them. Talking about books together is a great way to do this. Reading aloud and sharing books in an interactive way, rather than just reading the story straight through from start to finish, engages children more in thinking about the story and develops their vocabulary at the same time.

3. **Decide on age-appropriate activities to model.** Remember to think fun and engaging. *Example:* Use a picture book and model for the participants how to discuss the title and cover together. Pick a few stopping points to model predicting what will happen next, talking about the characters or events and how they relate to the child. Make it more fun by having a copresenter or workshop participant play the part of a child interacting with you about the story.

4. **Pick one activity for guided practice with participants.** *Example:* Have participants choose a partner. Distribute picture books and sticky notes to each pair, and give them time to pick stopping points in the story for predictions and possible questions.

After a small group activity, a participant volunteers to share with the larger group what they learned.

5. **Plan time to discuss how the activities fit into participants' learning environments.** Think about how you will encourage a rich discussion. *Example:* Allow time for groups to share and chart their ideas. Invite participants to role-play their book discussions, with one or more of them taking the part of the child responding to the prediction questions. As in step 3, this provides an opportunity for thinking about "childlike responses" the children in their care might give.

This basic model allows the transfer of learning we know is so important. Transfer of learning is the application of skills, knowledge, and attitudes that were learned in one situation to another situation, such as the participants' early literacy environments. Best practices in early literacy development may involve a shift in thinking for your workshop participants, so the more time they have to practice the activities, the more likely they will be to use them in their own setting.

Thinking from a Child's Point of View

During the workshop, some activities are geared toward children. Asking participants to think in a childlike way and play the part of a child during an activity in a school readiness workshop serves an important purpose. Not only does it set a light, playful tone for the training, it also encourages adults to see the activities from a child's point of view. This experience can cause an "ah-ha" moment for your workshop participants, as they recognize the value in the activity you are sharing with them. Ideally, it will encourage adults to want to go back and try the activities with their children to see if their reaction matches the children's.

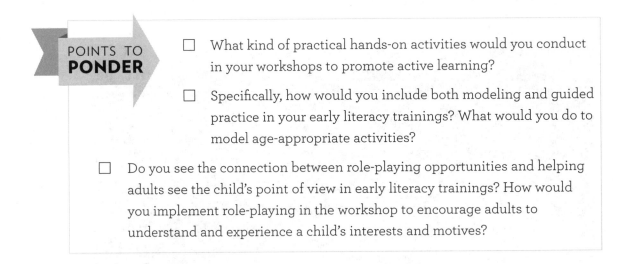

POINTS TO **PONDER**

☐ What kind of practical hands-on activities would you conduct in your workshops to promote active learning?

☐ Specifically, how would you include both modeling and guided practice in your early literacy trainings? What would you do to model age-appropriate activities?

☐ Do you see the connection between role-playing opportunities and helping adults see the child's point of view in early literacy trainings? How would you implement role-playing in the workshop to encourage adults to understand and experience a child's interests and motives?

NOTE

1. Catherine E. Snow, M. Susan Burns, and Peg Griffin, *Starting Out Right: A Guide to Promoting Children's Reading Success* (Washington, DC: National Academies Press, 1999).

The Power of Workshops

Some of the benefits of a face-to-face workshop are the opportunities to present information, to share demonstrations, and to provide hands-on activities and feedback. This is an important part of our holistic approach to training—workshops, materials, and follow-up support. The workshop experience offers a great opportunity for personal discussion and building trust with training participants. By creating meaningful dialogue with participants, librarians are also learning. Face-to-face communication establishes a critical foundation to overall communication.[1] This sets in motion a series of steps toward rapid growth of understanding, as well as a higher performance of fostering school readiness.

Show Respect. Caregivers, whether they are parents, grandparents, or child care professionals, need to understand the importance of their role in raising young children. The internationally renowned "Parents as Teachers" program (www.parentsasteachers.org) emphasizes that parents should be their child's first and best teacher. Child care providers can spend ten to twelve hours each weekday with the children in their care, which establishes their important influence

The first duty of love is to listen.
—PAUL TILLICH

in early learning. By showing that librarians understand their responsibilities and challenges, we help increase their comfort level in the training program. Participants are more willing to learn new things and to take reasonable risks when librarians convey the value of the roles of parents and child care professionals. Participants become more enthusiastic about engaging in sharing and discussion.

Set the Right Tone. Remember to strive for a friendly, but businesslike, tone. This actually starts with first contact when participants are signing up for the training, whether registration is done by phone or online. Convey respect and an upbeat attitude. Through verbal feedback and interaction, encourage everyone, no matter what their level of knowledge and skill at the start of the training program, to be their best self in the learning process.

Many parents lead hectic lives between work and family. Librarians can help alleviate parents' doubts and questions: "What should I do to help my child become ready for school?" "I'm not sure what is expected." "I don't have the time to teach my child to be ready for kindergarten." We can show parents many easy, yet meaningful ways to engage their children in learning through play. Parents see that the activities are fun and do not have to be time consuming.

Many child care professionals are frustrated and discouraged by perceptions that they are babysitters. By respecting their profession as child care experts, librarians can ease their concerns: "What am I already doing that is working?" "How can I expand my skills and goals in a reasonable yet effective time frame?" "How can I convince parents that I'm knowledgeable and skilled at helping their children become ready for school?" We can help answer these questions and guide child care professionals to increase their skills and repertoire, thereby increasing their self-confidence.

Hands-on Experiences in the Workshop

A powerful aspect of workshops is that they can serve as a venue for meaningful learning through hands-on activities and experiences. These experiences

- Build confidence in using techniques and activities being encouraged for use with children in the child care setting

- Promote an understanding of the fun of learning

- Encourage the expansion of activities with children, particularly in connection with language and literacy development from sharing stories and books

- Stimulate an understanding of a child's interest and curiosity about their environment, themselves, their feelings, and others around them

- Encourage use of props with storytime

- Provide opportunities for building relationships and a learning community with peers

- Provide information to strengthen participants' knowledge base and resources for further reference and use

Another benefit of the workshops is that the setting allows for more personal and powerful face-to-face communication. Communication is a two-way street. In a workshop atmosphere, you can build rapport in a more personal way, especially by evincing the trust and respect already mentioned. Additionally, you have an opportunity to hear firsthand the concerns, questions, and needs of your participants in order to better focus your efforts. Knowledge acquired through communicative interaction can lead to learning about other possibilities to consider in supporting mutual goals—by offering further training, providing library services, and so on.

Face-to-face communication builds credibility for your expertise and information you are sharing. In-person communications enhance motivation because your partners are able to see and hear your commitment and enthusiasm for the project. The workshops provide opportunities for real-time responses to questions and clarification; sometimes caregivers have been frustrated by contradictory or confusing information gained elsewhere. Finally, the communication of information by printed handouts and resource lists provides valuable and convenient references that can be referred back to after completion of the workshop.

Child Care Professionalism

Early childhood development and education experts agree that professional development is key to the quality of child care. Your state may have an office of child care with credentialing regulations that include professional development requirements. In Maryland this office comes under the auspices of the state Department of Education's Early Learning Division and sets standards, policy, and procedures to ensure high-quality child care training. Our library is an approved "training institute." The approval process does not take a great deal of time or effort, but it ensures that our early literacy trainings meet standards of quality for adult learning principles and knowledge content areas. In addition, it makes our trainings marketable to the child care community because the providers receive approved credit hours (*see web extra 1*).

In addition to credit hours, child care professionals are required to earn a certain number of professional units each year. By making a request to the Early Learning Division, our library was able to offer a professional unit for each participant who went above and beyond in their efforts to engage parents in their child's learning. Participants demonstrated to the librarian, through a brief verbal or written report, the activities they completed in this area—for example, sending home newsletters describing what parents can do to continue their child's learning on a specific topic or talking to parents one-on-one at the end of the day and encouraging them to conduct specific activities at home (*see web extra 2*).

POINTS TO
PONDER

☐ Do you actively communicate respect for participants in your workshops?

☐ How does someone's attitude toward you affect how you view or relate to that person?

☐ Take some time to reflect on the tone you set in your trainings. Is it friendly, upbeat, and professional?

NOTE

1. Chuck Martin, "The Importance of Face-to-Face Communication at Work," CIO, 2007, www.cio.com/article/29898/The_Importance_of_Face_to_Face_Communication_at_Work?page=1.

PART III

A Step-by-Step Guide to a Great Training Package

CHAPTER 7

Planning and Preparation

In planning for a workshop, always keep your goals in mind. Your overall goal is to promote school readiness. In adapting the ideas in this book to your program, remember that our results were based on Carroll County Public Library's research study. You should pick and choose for your own program. A solid training package

Let our advance worrying become advance thinking and planning.
—WINSTON CHURCHILL

· Engages caregivers and parents to be involved in the child's learning

· Focuses on conversation, book sharing, and play

· Uses everyday materials, books, and hands-on activities

· Is fun for adults and children

A little bit of planning goes a long way.

By taking time to create your ideal vision, you lay a strong foundation for your training program. Draft a realistic time line, one that works for you and your staff. Our library's study indicated that a take-home kit of school readiness materials gives participants the opportunity to conduct activities and share books with their children. This accelerates their ability to apply what they learned in the workshops. Community partners may be a source of financial support, free materials, promotion, and recruiting of participants. In addition, be sure to support your message with numerous handouts. Read on for more details to help you each step of the way.

Initial Planning, Including Administration and Community Buy-In

School readiness is a goal that many in your community can understand, so it is easy for them to recognize the potential for a training program. You are trying to help your library play a larger role in your community. By taking the time to think through the following points and gather information, you gain what you need to explain succinctly to administrators and partners why you are proposing this training.

- Dream big while setting realistic goals. Complete the following statement to articulate your vision. My training program idea is . . .

- Identify two or three key administrators to get on board. What are the best ways to gain their support? Identify two or three staff members who can be on your project team. Expect the time it takes to plan and prepare the training to range between two and fifteen hours a month, depending on the size of the project and the people involved.

- How will the training fulfill your library's mission statement and strategic plan?

- Identify community needs for such training. Who will be the targeted audience? Home child care providers? Parents? Non-English-speaking parents? What training, if any, is already offered to providers and parents?

- What are your audience's needs? Does your state or local education department have kindergarten assessment standards? If so, what is the percentage of children in your community entering school ready to succeed? What is the percentage of providers in your community trained in school readiness and early literacy? How many Title I schools are there? How can you reach out to providers and parents in those schools?

- How will the program meet the needs of the targeted audience? Describe the benefits. Use Carroll County Public Library's research study results to make your case. Incorporate research data on school readiness and child development.

- What other organizations work with this audience? What potential funding sources have similar goals? Examples include child care agencies, schools, businesses supporting literacy, community organizations, nonprofits, and government.

> You need to capture the enthusiasm you have for early literacy and school readiness and convey it. Our motto is *Be relentlessly proactive and cheerful!*

- Who in the library needs to be involved? What kinds of skills and expertise are needed? What will be the roles/responsibilities of your team? Who needs to be kept informed? How will you promote the training program?

- What other facts would be helpful in promoting your program, especially as you involve community partners and seek monetary support?

- How will you measure success?

- How will you adapt the program? St. Mary's County (Maryland) Public Library did not make phone calls to child care professionals but did follow up with visits by their WOW! (Words on Wheels) van to deliver storytimes and books. We have adapted our early literacy program to train Carroll County Spanish-speaking parents by scheduling two shorter Saturday morning workshops in the fall instead of the suggested four-hour workshop to accommodate family needs.

KEY POINTS ON PLANNING

☐ Carroll County Public Library's research study showed that the early literacy training package conducted by librarians had a positive impact on children's skills. There was a statistically significant increase in comprehension, phonological awareness, and concepts about print. A study implication is that, using a similar training program with a similar population, other libraries should get similar results.

☐ Research shows that children entering kindergarten developmentally ready in all areas are more likely to be ready to learn and be successful throughout their school years.

☐ Libraries and librarians can be an important free resource in providing information and assisting parents and child care providers with their young children's growth, particularly in language and literacy.

☐ Our plan is to help every child in our community become ready to succeed in school. One of the best ways to do that is to reach parents and caregivers. Parents are considered to be their child's first and best teacher, but they often need information and support to help them be successful. By training child care providers, we indirectly reach multiple children and their parents.

☐ An implication of Carroll County's study is that having a training package with take-home resources and ongoing support made a difference in the participants' ability to foster school readiness with the children in their care.

☐ Keep in mind that successful projects are usually accomplished by working as a team one step at a time.

☐ Develop a high-performing team. Choose team members or sounding board colleagues based on the needs of the training program. Create enthusiasm about the program. Define roles for each member. Tap into the knowledge and expertise of each member.

☐ As you develop your planning details and set your priorities, ask your project team members or sounding board colleagues to play devil's advocate by asking questions such as "Why are we doing *a*?" "Why did we choose *b*?" "Have we thought about *c*, *d*, or *e*?"

Estimating Your Budget Needs

Before submitting your proposal to administrators, be sure to estimate your program costs. Determine which activity cards you will use. The Ready At Five School Readiness Activity Cards we use are free to download or available for purchase from the Ready At Five website (www.readyatfive.org/raf/for-parents/activity-cards.html). You can also create your own cards using resources from ALA or other sources. Decide what play materials and supplies you will need for hands-on activities. When selecting activity cards, look for those that suggest interactive, age-appropriate, hands-on type activities in the various domains. Develop strategies to secure funding to purchase books and materials to give workshop participants a take-home kit at the initial workshop. Our research study implications show that supplying a kit of ready-to-use materials along with ongoing support makes a huge difference to participants' ability to foster school readiness.

Based on these plans, evaluate how much monetary support you need. We have been able to conduct the program on a modest budget by purchasing books along with a smaller percentage of kit resources. When purchasing for child care professionals, you may scale back on some items because some resources, such as washable markers and glue sticks, are usually a part of their teaching activities. When purchasing for parents, you may want to include most of the kit contents, since not all parents have everything on hand. If necessary, modify the kit to include materials from only a select number of the activity cards, especially language and literacy, depending on budget constraints.

We utilized low-cost resources from online and local dollar stores and other discount retailers, along with resources from community partners. For example, check with your local fire department for free children's firefighter hats to be used for pretend play. How large will your training group be? We recommend twelve to twenty-five participants for optimal training results.

- Determine your take-home kit contents and container or bag. How many books and materials can be purchased or found through donations? Can your purchasing department buy books and materials at a discount? Are other materials better purchased through discount stores and online venues?

- Will you have additional educational resources to send with the newsletters and offer in the follow-up workshop?

- Will you need to obtain supplies for workshop activities?

- Identify any additional general training supplies you will need, such as sticky notes, flip charts, markers, and binders.

TIPS FOR GRANT FUNDING AND FINDING SPONSORSHIPS

☐ Research the Foundation Center (http://foundationcenter.org) to find, for example, local individuals who have left money in their will for literacy. These funds are often administered by local banks.

☐ Inquire at national chain stores in your community, such as Target, Walmart, and Dollar General, about small grant opportunities.

☐ Ask local businesses for financial and volunteer support, including local banks.

☐ Find out who in your community contributes to early literacy and literacy projects, such as local service organizations, including Rotary clubs.

Budget scenarios might include books and materials for a take-home kit ($100–$200 per person); refreshments ($2–$4 per person per workshop); additional educational resources ($25–$75 per person); and start-up workshop supplies ($15–$75). What else will you need to spend money on? Some training programs include mailing out additional materials and end-of-program gifts such as a puppet. If yours does, you will need money for those materials and postage.

Keep a checklist of sponsors contacted, the date, and their response. You can use a chart to record your actual funds, your donations, and in-kind services. Who will be involved in purchases and recordkeeping—supervisors, staff, finance department?

Community Partners

How can you tap into the power of collaboration? Partners can support the program by helping to pay for materials, finding other monetary support, and assisting with activities for children in conjunction with parent workshops.

Partners can also encourage and facilitate attendance and provide space for your trainings. Identify three key community partners. When you have your partners on board, agree on the specific ways each partner will support your project. Open and positive communication can help address any issues that may arise during the program.

Congratulations!

You have gained approval from library administration and you have community partners on board. You have a projected budget and made some decisions about activity cards, books, and materials. Ideally you will form a team with a project director and one or two trainers working together for planning, presenting, and implementing the training package. If you are unable to form a team, there may be colleagues who are willing to act as sounding boards as you develop your training. Effective sounding boards are people willing to listen and give you open and thoughtful feedback. This can be especially important early on to bring different perspectives to the program.

Timing

The ideal time frame for implementation of the training package is to follow the school year. This allows you to relate your activities authentically to preparing the children for school. It adds a layer of credibility and emphasizes the important relationship between school readiness and school success. Also, the summer months may be disruptive because of vacations of providers and families.

Programming Logistics

Focusing on a few other details can make a world of difference in the final program:

- What assignments will each team member be responsible for during each phase of the project?
- What ideas do you have for making the workshop room colorful and exciting? Examples include using colored plastic tablecloths and displaying the kit of materials.
- Where will you hold the workshops? Who is responsible for booking, setup, breakdown?
- Will you offer light refreshments to provide a welcoming atmosphere and an energy boost during the workshop? Will there be food available before the workshop begins and at the break, appropriate for the time of day the workshop is presented? Who will be responsible for purchasing and setting up refreshments? Note: Many grants do not cover the cost of refreshments.

- Who will be responsible for the application process for obtaining state licensing of clock hours for the training? Who will issue Continuing Education Unit credentials?

- When will you send confirmation letters? Will you keep a waiting list? Who will keep a record of attendees?

Recruiting Participants

The recruiting process is a time to draw on your community partners to help promote your training. They can be an excellent resource for connecting potential participants to your training. Attending established meetings, such as a child care association meeting, a Head Start parent meeting, or a young mother's group, can be a cost-effective way to recruit.

Early in your process, learn the clock hour approval process for child care provider workshops. Apply for approval through your state's child care administration. Earning training clock hours toward licensing can be an important motivation for participation.

Find Out What Participants Know

As one of the assessment components of our research design, we conducted surveys. We used a preprogram survey to assess background knowledge and use of best practices. Such information helps you target your efforts toward participants' needs. The post-survey information provides program effectiveness to share with stakeholders, which may help secure future funding (*see web extras 3 and 4*).

WAYS TO MEASURE PROGRAM SUCCESS

- ☐ Outcome-based evaluation that demonstrates a change in a skill, knowledge, attitude, or behavior, for example, x percent of participants show an increase in their early literacy knowledge and y percent of their children ages a to b demonstrate growth in print awareness and narrative skills

- ☐ Anecdotal examples and activity samples that demonstrate growth in school readiness

- ☐ Verbal and written reports from participants

- ☐ Attendance

- ☐ Pre- and post-surveys

- ☐ Workshop feedback using "quick-writes" or other written evaluations

Prepare Workshop Materials

Remember to organize your hands-on activity supplies/handouts for easy distribution during the workshop. The following lists of recommended books and materials should help you put together your take-home kits (*see web extra 5*). We used suppliers such as Lakeshore Learning, Discount School Supplies, Walmart, and various dollar stores.

WORKSHOP READY AT FIVE KIT MATERIALS

- ☐ activity balls
- ☐ baby doll
- ☐ bag of foam shapes
- ☐ bean bags
- ☐ chenille stems
- ☐ child's aprons
- ☐ colored bowls
- ☐ construction paper
- ☐ Counting Bears math game
- ☐ crayons
- ☐ doctor's kit
- ☐ dry erase boards
- ☐ dry erase markers
- ☐ fake orange feathers
- ☐ firefighter hat
- ☐ flashlight/batteries
- ☐ glue sticks
- ☐ hole punch
- ☐ ice cube tray
- ☐ jump rope
- ☐ kid's scissors
- ☐ magnetic letters, upper- and lowercase
- ☐ magnets (horseshoe or wand)
- ☐ magnifying glasses
- ☐ measuring cups/spoons
- ☐ memory game
- ☐ mirror sheets
- ☐ multicultural crayons
- ☐ musical instruments
- ☐ play money and play coins
- ☐ pompoms
- ☐ scarves
- ☐ science bag (Sink or Float items such as seashells and Styrofoam balls)
- ☐ sidewalk chalk
- ☐ smelly stickers, orange and strawberry
- ☐ tea set
- ☐ washable glitter glue
- ☐ washable markers
- ☐ yarn

WORKSHOP BOOKS

Alexander and the Terrible, Horrible, No Good, Very Bad Day by Judith Viorst

Baby Faces by Margaret Miller

Brown Rabbit's Shape Book by Alan Baker

Chicka Chicka Boom Boom by Bill Martin Jr.

Counting Kisses by Karen Katz

Goldilocks and the Three Bears by Jan Brett

The Grouchy Ladybug by Eric Carle

The Little Red Hen by Paul Galdone

The Mitten by Jan Brett

My Very First Mother Goose by Iona Opie

One Fish, Two Fish, Red Fish, Blue Fish by Dr. Seuss.

Pat the Bunny by Dorothy Kunhardt

Ten Little Ladybugs by Melanie Gerth

The Three Billy Goats Gruff by Janet Stevens

The Very Hungry Caterpillar by Eric Carle

Wash Your Hands by Tony Ross

We're Going on a Bear Hunt by Helen Oxenbury

In our library, we have take-home kit-collating parties with staff and volunteers to organize the books into tote bags and the activity materials into plastic tubs for easy transporting. It's a time in which others in your organization and community can help children become ready for school.

POINTS TO **PONDER**

☐ After reading the tips for recruiting participants, did you think about possible participants who would benefit from the training package?

☐ Were you able to think of ways to adapt the training package to what you are already doing and to your particular situation?

☐ How does the suggested time line, presented so far, fit in with your plans/commitments?

CHAPTER 8

The Primary Workshop

Once you have planned your overall training program, it is time to prepare your goals for the initial or primary workshop. This workshop is the heart of your training program, motivating your audience to inspire children to learn. The model presented is specific to child care professionals and parents, but it can be adapted for many audiences including grandparents and Head Start teachers.

The workshop is designed to promote school readiness by increasing participants' understanding of best practices. Your role is to motivate adults to have more intentional interaction with children. Adults can become empowered and see themselves as knowledgeable professionals and parents. The workshop provides engaging hands-on experiences to encourage the use of modeled behaviors. Practice along with discussion creates a springboard for learning.

For our project, we used activities on the Ready At Five School Readiness Activity Cards, which can be downloaded for free or purchased for a modest amount (www.readyatfive.org/raf/for-parents/activity-cards.html). The cards are geared toward children three and four years old, but they can easily be adapted to infants and toddlers or to even older children. No matter which activity cards or activities

If you want your children to be intelligent, read them fairy tales. If you want them to be more intelligent, read them more fairy tales.
—ALBERT EINSTEIN

you choose, they can be modified to suit the age of the child. The Ready At Five website and the Zero to Three website (www.zerotothree.org) are practical sources to help you and participants understand how to adapt and create activities. Bear in mind that children learn at different rates. What is appropriate for one 24-month-old's level of learning in a particular area may be slightly different from another 24-month-old's.

For our workshop we provided a take-home kit of books and resources that would facilitate using the Ready At Five activity cards. The kit materials may vary from library to library. The important part is that you are providing some materials to motivate the participants and enhance their transfer of learning.

The ideal season for this workshop, especially if you are implementing the entire training package, is in the fall (September or October) near the start of the school year. We use a time frame from 9 a.m. to 1 p.m. on a Saturday for professionals and 10 a.m. to 12 noon on a Saturday for parents. We offer snacks to keep participants energized throughout the workshop (see appendix C, web extra 6). Prepare and present in a way that the learners ponder what the information means to them and how it applies to their specific situations. In this chapter we provide a sample agenda with suggested time allotments as a guide.

The Workshop: A Step at a Time

Tips for Success

- **Do**—create the workshop in a style and manner you are comfortable with.
- **Do**—think of yourself sharing information with friends and coworkers as opposed to giving a lecture or speech.
- **Do**—express your excitement and belief in the importance of the information.
- **Do**—build rapport with participants and create an upbeat tone.
- **Do**—tap into the enthusiasm and goodwill of fellow trainers to present a united team.
- **Do**—look for opportunities to present how the information applies to participants' specific situation.
- **Do**—keep the atmosphere comfortable by interjecting light moments as appropriate.
- **Do**—start and end your workshop on time.
- **Do**—plan ahead to make up any part of the workshop that may go over the allotted time (e.g., shorten the break, condense or cut sections of the presentation).
- ***Do not**—make participants feel rushed if you are running short on time.*
- **Do**—make adjustments as needed for successful timing, and keep the tone light and positive.

- **Do**—use simple statements, such as "We have two more minutes to finish this activity" or "We have time for one more idea or suggestion. Table 3 [call on group that hasn't given input yet], what is your group's best input on this?"

- **Do**—remain flexible. One key to successful timing is cooperation and support between trainers, who should be cognizant of the time and give simple nonverbal cues about when time is getting close to the end of a segment.

- **Do**—use PowerPoint slide shows, flip charts, whiteboards, or other methods of providing a visual of the information.

- **Do**—provide information in a binder, folder, or as separate handouts to help participants focus on your presentation instead of taking voluminous notes; some note taking is helpful.

- **Do**—tape small posters with school readiness tips onto the walls and refer to them during the workshop.

I. **Welcome, Introductions, Housekeeping, Peer Coaching/Feedback (10 minutes total)**

A. *Welcome*

The way you begin can help establish a learning atmosphere and start building relationships between trainers and participants. Create a tone that is professional yet relaxed, upbeat yet sincere, and encourages two-way sharing yet stays on task.

Colored tablecloths and school readiness posters on the walls can enhance the learning environment (*see web extras 7–13*).

Talking Points

- We are glad you are here! The library honors your commitment to your children. Our common goal is to help children become school ready.

- We know that you have a strong commitment to your children because you have taken your personal time to participate in this training program.

- [For child care providers] We recognize that you are a professional. We also know that you may not be recognized as such by parents, public officials, and others. You may be viewed by others as glorified babysitters. We understand the challenges and responsibilities you face as you inspire children to learn and help them develop. This workshop is designed to support your professional growth and provide some ideas and information to make your role easier and more beneficial to your children.

- [For parents] We recognize that you are already doing wonderful things for your child. You, like many parents, lead busy and full lives. This workshop is designed to support you as a parent and provide some ideas and information to make your role easier and more beneficial to your children.

B. *Introductions*

The project director can quickly introduce himself or herself and the other trainer(s), or trainers may introduce themselves. Give a brief statement of your professional background that is relevant to your credentials for presenting workshops. This may include why you are enthusiastic and committed to this project. If there is time, some brief piece of personal information can help build connections with participants.

C. *Housekeeping*

Housekeeping explains the parameters for conducting the workshop and logistics.

Talking Points

- We start and end workshops on time.
- Be comfortable. Feel free to get up and help yourself to refreshments [if available], use the restroom, stretch or move around, as necessary.
- The restrooms are located [indicate where].
- There will be a break during the workshop.
- We don't have all the answers to your questions, but we are providing information based on research, our professional experience, and knowledge of best practices.
- Our emphasis, as librarians, is in the area of language and literacy.
- This is *your* workshop. We want it to be interactive. Please ask questions if there is something that isn't clear. Please share your ideas for what has worked well with your children. Remember: the success of your children is your success.

D. *Peer Coaching*

Briefly explain the concept of peer coaching and have a handout (*web extra 14*) ready for distribution.

Talking Points

- We are passing out a handout that describes the simple steps for using a peer coaching method. The goal is to improve your techniques and skills through peer feedback and support.
- Peer coaching is a mutual relationship in which two or more people agree to help each other apply new skills.
- Research suggests that 10 percent of workshop participants transfer new skills into practice through theory and demonstration. Twenty-five percent transfer new skills into practice through theory, demonstration, practice within the training, and feedback from the instructor. If a peer

coaching component is added, the transfer of new skills increases to 90 percent of workshop participants.

- We encourage you to call or e-mail each other. Please discuss how a new activity went, if anything could have been done differently to improve results if you felt it did not go as well as you hoped, and to see if you both had similar results for the same activity.

II. Goals and Learning Philosophy (5 minutes total)

A. Goals

Present workshop goals by reading through them with brief explanations. Have the goals easily visible for participants to view as you present them.

Talking Points

- You will learn about the developmental areas or domains of early learning—personal and social development, language and literacy, social studies, mathematics, science, physical development, and the arts—and you will learn about developmentally appropriate expectations for children entering kindergarten.
- You will learn techniques for developing school readiness in your child care setting or at home through the use of activities and resources.
- You will focus on learning to use activities provided and to create new age-appropriate activities to develop skills in the language and literacy learning domain by sharing information, resources, and hands-on learning activities.
- [For child care providers] You will explore and implement ways to encourage parental involvement to support development of their children's school readiness skills at home.

B. Learning Philosophy

Introduce the learning philosophy concept and post the principles on a flip chart or PowerPoint presentation.

Talking Points: You Are Responsible for Your Own Learning

- Learning activities can occur anywhere and under any circumstance to increase our knowledge, to enhance a skill, and to adapt to change. Each of us can strive to become a lifelong learner by consistently evaluating what worked well and what we could have done differently in a situation to produce better results. We encourage you to be active lifelong learners by taking advantage of formal and informal learning opportunities, seeking challenges and intellectual stimulation, taking reasonable risks to try something new, tapping into your curiosity, and reinforcing what you learn by sharing information with others.

- As an example, you might not normally gravitate to the topic of science, but you read a magazine article about the rapidly growing biotechnology industry. This in turns galvanizes your efforts to help your children develop scientific thinking skills.

- We strongly encourage you to take advantage of ways to reinforce your own learning during today's workshop:

  We've provided sticky notes/note pads and pens/pencils for you to make notes to yourself to put in the picture books and binder/folder.

  Please take advantage of the small group activities today to share ideas and information with other participants.

  Use the opportunity, when the small groups report back to the whole group, to learn from others and to think about how your children would respond to the activities and stories.

  Participants in other workshops reported that this time for sharing is an excellent chance to problem-solve, discuss, and share with peers.

Talking Points: The Power of the "See It, Do It, Teach It" Approach

- Have you ever had the experience of learning something new, trying it for yourself, and then sharing your excitement (and perhaps frustration) with others who were also acquiring this same new skill? Reinforced learning is a powerful tool, but one that requires more than a one-shot workshop.

- This is why our training package provides ongoing support in the form of phone calls, online contact with us and with your peers, along with newsletters and a follow-up workshop. We want to provide opportunities to extend your learning and to share what went well and what didn't quite go as planned when you try new things.

- Research shows the importance of adults in helping children succeed by demonstrating the power of inspiration ("Eureka!"); through personal interaction and attention to the child; by modeling behaviors; by building trust, confidence, and self-esteem and letting the children know they are special; and by making learning fun!

III. **Share School Readiness Information through an Introduction to Resources (Handouts, Binder, or Online Access via a wiki, blog, or Ning), Activity Cards and Kit, Hands-on Science Experience, and Pretend Play Activity (45 minutes total)**

A. *Overview*

Child care professionals and parents need and desire reference information related to school readiness and child development. Whether you are providing handouts or an information binder or creating your own online resources—or doing all three—introduce each topic for their reference use.

Talking Points

- The binder or folder can be a place to begin creating your own library of resources. Please add to it as you read articles, attend other trainings, and explore online resources. We have also created an online wiki for a way to find additional links and articles. The table of contents provides quick reference to the various sections:

Sample Table of Contents for the Information Binder

1. Contents of Ready At Five kit

2. Brain research/multiple intelligences

3. School readiness learning domains

4. Pretend play and social/emotional development

5. Language and literacy domain

6. Suggested book and music lists

7. Fingerplays/flannelboard patterns/other resources

8. Parent involvement resources

Talking Points: Brain Development

- Since the 1990s there have been major technical and procedural advancements, such as MRIs, PET scans, and testing strategies for behaviors, that have transformed our understanding of brain development. Discoveries include new breakthroughs in cognitive learning and social/emotional development in young children birth to five. As a result, we have learned that approximately 80 percent of brain growth takes place in the first three years of life, that a combination of nature and nurture contribute to how a baby's brain works, and that there are optimal learning periods in the early years called "windows of opportunity" that are the best times to gain information and develop specific skills.

- Neurons (brain cells) need to establish connections to each other for the brain to build knowledge and control functions such as making decisions, managing emotions, and solving problems. These connections increase and are strengthened through experiences after birth.

- The brain develops in a specific order. This is a basic overview of brain functioning. Zero to Three and other resources provide more in-depth information.

  First, the brainstem is responsible for making sure the body is functioning, such as breathing, developing a heart rate, swallowing, and sleeping.

  Second, the limbic system develops. This is often referred to as the emotional part of the brain.

Third, the cortex, associated with higher brain functioning, develops. It is the cognitive, or thinking, part of the brain. It is essential for emotional management, language abilities, decision making, and reasoning.

If a child does not develop healthy emotional responses and control, it is much more difficult for the "thinking" part of the brain to learn, develop language skills, express empathy, or develop problem-solving skills.

- Here is a quote from the book *Making Connections: Teaching and the Human Brain:* "Preschool and early elementary school years are sometimes referred to as 'the wonder years of learning' because so much learning and building of neural connections for communication within the brain are continuing to be built and reinforced." Notice the word wonder, which also relates to curiosity. Fostering curiosity and active engagement makes learning fun.

Talking Points: Social/Emotional Development

- The most important factor in developing healthy social/emotional development is the positive, loving attachment between the primary caregiver and the child.

- [For child care providers] We know you often spend more time with some of the children in your care than do their parents. You are also their caregiver during the most active, experiential parts of their day.

- Bonding between adult and child is built on the loving responses you provide as you interact with a child. Remember to respond verbally to cues that signal a child's emotions and interests, continually demonstrating that the child is special and important to you. Don't forget to use appropriate touch such as rocking infants, holding, and hugging. Listen to children as well as talk to them. Sing, read, and play together.

- [For child care providers] Studies show that secure attachment to a child's first child care provider predicted a child's ability to have a trusting relationship with teachers and success in school. Emotion can't be separated from cognitive learning. Emotion motivates us to learn and to create.

- The window of opportunity for learning to manage impulses and emotions is between the ages of two and five years. How well these skills develop depends to a large extent on having a caring adult available to model, guide, and support self-regulation.

- Adults play a primary role in helping children to identify, name, and respond to emotions in themselves and others. It can be beneficial to have some basic knowledge or references about a child's progression through the ages and stages of emotional and social development, especially in helping them understand and describe feelings to others and to gain control of their feelings. Some examples of issues in these years are fear, anger, frustration, and developing empathy and the willingness to share.

- As the saying goes, "If you have their hearts, you'll have their minds." In other words, if you have a close, loving, trusting relationship with a child, they will be more willing to experience and learn new things with you.

- Pretend play is unstructured, imagining play. It is through play that children learn. Play is essential for positive childhood development. We'll explore pretend play in more detail later in the workshop.

Talking Points: School Readiness Skills

- How prepared a child is to enter school ready and willing to learn is a key indicator of how successful that child will be throughout the school years.

- Because research has shown this factor to be important, the Maryland State Department of Education hired professionals to identify key areas for well-rounded development and to create assessment tools to determine each child's readiness in those areas at the beginning of kindergarten. These are aligned with general national standards.

- Seven areas of development were identified in Maryland as key to school success and are standard areas, or domains, of learning: social/emotional development, physical development, language and literacy, mathematical thinking, scientific thinking, social studies, and the arts.

Talking Points: Parental Participation [Child Care Professional Workshop]

- One way to build effective relationships with parents is to share scientific research and brain development information with them.

- We encourage you to share information about how you as a professional are promoting their child's development.

During the break, trainer Dianne Black invites participants to explore the display of kit books and materials in front of the room.

- You can recommend that parents continue the activities and learning process at home.

B. *Materials and Resources*

Talking Points: Ready At Five Activity Cards and Take-Home Kit Contents

- [Display any take-home resources or kits you are providing participants.] The Ready At Five cards are provided to give you easy-to-follow, age-appropriate activities to promote school readiness in each of the seven domains we mentioned today.

- Our training focuses primarily on the language and literacy domain, but we review the other domains too. You will discover that the books and activities usually incorporate learning and skill development in more than one domain. Cards cover activities for all the learning domains but touch on language and literacy in some aspect to help children build vocabulary and background knowledge for the domain.

- The activity cards are going to help make learning fun for both you and your children.

- Activities can be readily adapted to fit the age and ability of your children. You know their abilities best, including strengths, developmental level, and issues affecting their learning and growth in skills.

- The activities on the cards can also lead to further exploration, gathering of information, and extension activities that are based on the children's interests and curiosity.

- It is important to use the cards and provided resources on a regular basis to promote repetition and foster learning. These activities are designed by experts to promote school readiness.

- [For child care providers] Share with parents that these activities are designed by experts to promote school readiness. They are sure to be impressed by the learning that is taking place on a daily basis.

- Today you will go back to your child care settings or home with books and learning materials at your fingertips to get started right away.

- These kit materials will allow you to engage in learning activities with your children. Many items listed on the cards may also be available in your child care or home. Most of the recommended books or similar titles can be found at your public library.

Talking Points: Book Lists and Resource Lists

- Librarians compiled these lists to suggest the best books to use with young children. Different types and themes of books are appropriate for different ages in the early years.

- Touch-and-feel, cardboard, and soft books promote an introduction and enjoyment of books for babies through toddlers.

- The preschool age is a time to begin to introduce nonfiction books also.

- The lists can also help with developing themes and skills, such as holidays, families, seasons, and problem solving.

Talking Points: Extension Resources and Activities

- This section contains sample rhymes, patterns, fingerplays, and other resources that are useful for fun and engaging learning. Some of the activities are themed for the "make-it, take-it" extension we will be making later.

- Rhythm, Rhyme, and Repetition are the 3 Rs of early literacy. Extension activities such as fingerplays, bounces and tickles, rhyming songs, music, flannelboards, stick puppets, and dramatic retelling all lend themselves to supporting the learning and skills promoted by the 3 Rs.

C. *Hands-on Science Activities*

Provide the materials to complete the Sink or Float activity and the Science Toolbox activity listed on the activity cards. Place one card and supplies for that activity at each table, so you have several tables experiencing each one. Provide a copy of our expanded sink/float chart (*web extra 15*) for each participant to take home. **TIP:** Because this is their first group activity and opportunity to use a learning tool, it is especially important for you to express enthusiasm, foster a sense of fun and discovery, and be reassuring about the ease of doing these activities.

Take the time to mix with participants and listen to their discussions during group activities; it builds rapport and gives you a better sense of how they are thinking. Sitting in on some conversations can help you determine whether participants understand what has been presented; it also provides an opportunity to be available for support and questions.

Talking Points

- Please use the instructions on the activity card and work together at your table to complete the activities listed on the front side of the card.

- As you conduct the activities, we encourage you to be childlike—not childish, of course—but to think from a child's viewpoint. The idea is to experience these activities as children. Think about and then discuss:

  How your children would respond to the activity

  What questions your children might ask

  What additional activities they might want to try

What rich language development can take place as the children explore the concepts of sinking and floating and use tools in different ways to learn

- These activities do a great job of promoting language development, especially introducing scientific terms, along with the scientific thinking needed for school readiness. For example, the Sink or Float activity introduces prediction and charting. It is best to use correct terms with children as they learn about science, math, and other fields. You can help them understand the terms on their level of comprehension.

- Hands-on experience leads to a child's understanding and holds the power of "discovery" learning.

- The Science Toolbox activity is excellent for introducing children to the concept of simple tools to explore and gather information about light, magnets, and magnification.

- Heads up! These activities are not shared with children as a "teaching" exercise or lesson. Remember that young children learn best through play, not through a formal lesson. School readiness activities are designed to be fun and tap a child's interest in topics and ideas. They help children gain a beginning sense of scientific thinking, mathematical thinking, and skills in all learning domains.

- All of the activities encourage conversation and expand vocabulary—which are critical factors for early literacy development.

- Please use the sticky notes provided at the tables to jot down any reminders you think would be important when you try this activity with the children in your care.

- As with any activity, *stop* when your child is no longer engaged and having fun. It will be a negative experience if the child or you is too tired, distracted, or not interested at that particular time.

After they complete the activities and discussion, ask participants at two tables (one for each of the two activity cards) to volunteer to share comments or observations about the activities.

Talking Points: Volunteers to Share

- Remember: there is no right or wrong answer as you do activities with children. They have active imaginations and are limited in their life experiences, so their answers are what *they* think or have problem-solved. It is an ongoing learning process, and the process is more important than right or wrong answers. You can direct their experience so they do understand what is correct information.

- Do we have a table willing to share some comments or observations about your activity?

D. Pretend Play Skit and Discussion

The pretend play skit, for three workshop trainers or one trainer and two volunteers, highlights how play can provide modeling and enrich conversation that extends learning for both children and the adult (see appendix D, web extra 16). It does not have to be presented word for word; it offers key actions and talking points in the dialogue to demonstrate different types of situations that provide interactive learning opportunities during pretend play.

Talking Points: Introducing the Pretend Play Skit

- Play is a child's work. It is through play that children learn.

- One goal is to help children develop cognitive learning skills. First encouraging and developing healthy social/emotional growth makes cognitive learning possible.

- Pretend play develops social/emotional skills, imagination, language, and problem-solving abilities.

- Research shows that children think more deeply about and stay longer with an activity when there is occasional adult interaction during play. This expands the learning experience.

- Children pay more attention to other learning experiences after they have had time for unstructured or pretend play.

- Through pretend play children can come to terms with their feelings, which is critical for healthy social/emotional growth.

- Over time, play helps children learn negotiation skills—including learning to delay gratification and consider the feelings and needs of others.

- Pretend play can help children learn from their mistakes without embarrassment or a sense of failure.

- A child's capacity and eagerness to engage in increasingly complex play are vital signs of healthy growth, emotionally, socially, and cognitively.

- This skit involves two young children interacting while playing doctor and their child care provider helping them to process their feelings. As you watch and listen, think about what the children are learning through pretend play and how the child care provider extends their learning through her conversation with them. Also observe ways that the caregiver learns more about the children and can gain ideas for other activities as follow-up, and how the caregiver can gauge stages of social development.

- Although the skit includes several types of interaction to show you a variety of examples, in real life adult interaction during pretend play should be only a brief occasional focused occurrence. Play is primarily for children to learn through interacting with each other.

Note the importance of keeping a sense of humor and using it with children, although this is easier said than done some days. Present the skit, and then follow up with discussion. As participants share their observations, integrate the following points about what was modeled in the skit if they don't volunteer them.

Talking Points: Discussing the Skit

- In this skit, you as child care provider observe and listen to children at play to learn about their current play interests and activities.

- You can use this information to extend and enrich the children's interests and learning opportunities: finding out about going to the doctor; having a parent (nurse, doctor) visit to talk with children and answer questions; maybe taking a field trip to a doctor or hospital; exploring careers in medicine by using nonfiction books and other resources, as age appropriate.

- The skit demonstrates how you can promote positive social/emotional skills, including empathy, understanding and management of feelings, and age-appropriate interactions with others.

- The skit allows caregivers to foster literacy skills by building vocabulary (e.g., explaining stethoscope), exploring beginning letters and sounds, and extending the children's learning by reading stories and nonfiction books about related subjects of interest. Prewriting skills could have also been encouraged by modeling writing a prescription for the baby.

IV. Early Literacy Development (40 minutes total)

Our workshop focuses on five key areas of early literacy development: vocabulary or language development, comprehension or narrative skills, letter knowledge, phonological awareness, and book and print awareness. In the activities we describe, we promote ALA's five key practices: talking, singing, reading, writing, and playing.

A. Early Literacy Development

Present the five areas of early literacy development covered in this workshop.

Talking Points: Building Language Skills

- You can help children build language skills in developmentally appropriate ways by singing together, talking together, playing labeling games, playing listening games, encouraging pretend play, and reading books together. Learning experiences in all of the domains provide opportunities for you to foster language development and build background knowledge. Language skills are the cornerstone of early literacy development.

Talking Points: Developing Comprehension

- You can develop early comprehension skills by reading many different types of books, including fiction and nonfiction, asking questions about the stories, encouraging children to talk about how the stories connect to what they already know, and encouraging children to retell stories with puppets, flannelboards, and other materials.

- The goal is to engage your children with the reading selections. By including both fiction and nonfiction at an early age, you are more likely to tap into the children's interests and foster that engagement.

Talking Points: Learning about Letters

- You can help children learn about letters in developmentally appropriate ways by sharing alphabet books, singing the alphabet song, giving children magnetic and foam letters to play with so they can explore letter shapes, helping children learn the letters in their name, and letting children experiment with writing.

- Learning about letters is part of developing an understanding of the alphabetic principle: letters represent sounds in words, and this is how we read and write.

- Children usually begin to experiment with writing by scribbling, and any efforts at using pencils or crayons are an important part of the ongoing learning process, as writing evolves over time.

Talking Points: Learning about Sounds in Words

- Developing phonological awareness, or learning to pay attention to the sounds in words, is an important component of early literacy development and is often called the "precursor" to phonics instruction (learning about letter/sound correspondence).

- It is a new concept for young children, since attention is focused on word meanings when they are first learning to speak. Happily, children usually love language play activities once they are introduced, so this is a particularly fun area of early literacy development to promote with your children.

- Children learn to pay attention to the sounds in words when you share nursery rhymes and poetry, share stories and songs that involve language play, play rhyming games, and clap syllables or word parts in words (pop-corn, can-dy). Remember, we are doing these activities orally (not connected to print).

- Classic nursery rhymes are a wonderful way to build this skill. Dr. Seuss is always a favorite as children grow older.

- One simple way to start emphasizing rhyming words is to recite a nursery rhyme or poem the children have heard several times before, then pause for them to contribute the rhyme. For example, One two, buckle my . . . Three, four, knock at the . . .

- Children love singing funny songs with language play, such as those by the children's performing artist Raffi and others [share your favorites].

- Older children (four- and five-year-olds) enjoy playing rhyming games such as I Spy (e.g., I spy something that rhymes with *hat*) and making up silly verses to songs. You can also play I Spy with beginning sounds (e.g., I spy something that starts with /t/). Another fun activity is simply clapping word parts (syllables): pop-corn (two claps), cup-cake (two claps), yes-ter-day (three claps).

- Your goal with these activities is simply to "tune children's ears" to the sounds in words, from larger units of sound (e.g., rhymes) to smaller units of sound (e.g., syllables and individual sounds). This helps prepare them for formal reading instruction once they enter school.

- Remember, these should always be fun activities that the children are enjoying. As with book sharing, let the children's responses be your guide, keep it brief, and stop if the children lose interest.

Talking Points: Learning about Books and Print

- Developing print awareness, or learning about books and print, happens easily in a print-rich environment. Children who are surrounded by books, read to often, and allowed to touch and handle books and experiment with writing develop the understandings about print that pave the way for reading success in school.

- Children learn about books and print when you read to them daily, talk about the cover of the book before reading the story, point to the title as you read it, occasionally point to the print while reading (being careful not to disrupt the flow of the story), choose their favorites, and call attention to print in their environment.

- A fun way to call attention to the front cover of the book versus the back cover is to hold up a book upside down and backward, pretend you are having trouble reading it, and ask children to tell you what's wrong. [Model with one of the books from the kit.] They will love "correcting you" and telling you to turn it around. Then you can say, "Oh, that's right, here's the front cover of the book. Let's look at the title (point to and read it aloud)." You can point out the author and illustrator and talk about what each one does. Before long, the children will be able to tell you this on their own. They will be able to recognize favorite books by their covers and may bring them to you to read again and again. This is a good behavior, for it is a sign that they are tuning in to the world of books and print and trying to "unlock the puzzle" it represents to them.

- Occasionally, when sharing a story, run your finger along the print as you read. You can also do this with any charts of poems, directions, or songs you may use in your child care setting. Around the age of four, most children begin to understand that the print is what you are reading. Before this age, you can also help develop this awareness that print conveys meaning by calling attention to print in their environment, such as a Cheerios box, a stop sign, or a McDonald's sign. You can include print as part of their pretend play centers (e.g., menus, shopping lists, writing paper and envelopes).

- Be sure to make time for children to experiment with writing as part of exploring the world of print. Their first attempts will probably be scribble, but that is an important first step. Just remember to praise all attempts, and show them how to write the letters in their name when they express an interest.

- Take this opportunity to promote whatever resources your library has to make books available.

B. *Reading Tips Ring*

A ring of reading tips and activities is included in the take-home kit to plan learning and enjoyment strategies for sharing read-aloud books (*see web extra 17*). Have a sample ring available to demonstrate during your talking points.

It is best if the tips are copied on card stock of two colors (one section of techniques for adults to choose from and one section of activities for children to choose from) and laminated, if possible, before attaching to a simple binder ring to ensure longer use. Promote enthusiasm for using this resource.

Reading tips ring

CARD 37—C

Comprehension

After reading a story, have your child tell you who the different characters (people, animals, etc.) were in the main story. Then ask if he can repeat all of them to you. This is helpful for children to gain story confidence and an understanding of the parts of a story.

Talking Points

- One of the resources prepared for this workshop is this reading tips ring. It is actually a collection of reminders, tips, and activities in two sections. One section has easy reminders of simple techniques and learning activities that you can select to use when introducing and reading stories. The second section has a variety of follow-up activity suggestions to engage children in the process of reading enjoyment and skill development.

- We hope you find this to be a useful resource as you begin to share books, both fiction and nonfiction, more interactively to foster language and literacy development. We suggest that you use the second section as a way of letting the children become more involved in activities related to the story by allowing one or more of them (such as the "friend of the day") to choose randomly from the cards to determine follow-up activities. Since the cards are attached to a simple metal ring, it is easy to fan them out for a child to make a selection. [Share a couple of examples from the second section by modeling fanning out the cards and having someone pick.]

- We recommend that you keep this ring handy for using when you share a read-aloud story with your children.

V. Best Practices for Sharing Books and Enhancing Learning Using Extension Activities (70 minutes total)

A. Demonstrate How to Share a Picture Book

Using *The Very Hungry Caterpillar* as a model, demonstrate how to share a picture book and extend the learning that can take place before, during, and after a read-aloud. Choose two or three volunteer participants to be your storytime audience as if they were in a home or child care setting.

Talking Points: How to Share a Picture Book

- In this part of the workshop, you have another opportunity to participate in an activity as children. Please experience the story sharing "through the eyes of a child."

- Making the story a shared experience or adventure is more beneficial to a child's learning than simply hearing a book read aloud.

- Sharing a story builds a bond between reader and listeners. Children love the warm ritual of being read to, and it is a great way to bond with them.

- Segue from introductory comments to beginning the storytime. Hold up the book to show the story you will be sharing.

Talking Points: Model the Story Sharing

- When you are sharing a book with children, you can ask, do you know what is on the cover of the book? You may have to help them identify the caterpillar; you may hear "worm," "snake," "crawly thing."

- Look what I have in my pocket (lap, basket, etc.). Now my caterpillar is hiding *behind* my knee, next he's crawling *up* my leg, now he's crawling *along* my arm, now he's going *over* my shoulder, and here he is *on top of* my head. Use a caterpillar puppet or a simple caterpillar you make.

- Now, let's pretend we all have our own caterpillar. Our pointer finger is our fuzzy caterpillar. Repeat the actions slowly as your finger "crawls" as you just did with your caterpillar puppet. Let's repeat together. Have the "children" repeat after you as the caterpillar makes his journey to the top of the head.

- Model best library and early literacy practices, as you begin to read the story aloud, by pointing to the words in the title as you read them: This is the title of the book—it tells us what the story is about. The author is Eric Carle, who wrote the story. The illustrator, who made the pictures, is also Eric Carle. Look at the back cover—we have a tiny caterpillar. Talk about the word "tiny" and how little the caterpillar looks in the picture.

- Ask questions that help them relate to the subject of the story: Have you ever seen or touched a caterpillar? If you have, how did it feel?

- Ask a predicting question: The title says the very hungry caterpillar. Do you think he will eat a lot in this story?

- Let's read the story to see what happens. Notice how I am using pacing and inflection while reading the story. Your children will be more engaged in the story when you do this too. Give it a try; it is fun.

- During the story, stop occasionally to ask questions: Can you help me count all the fruit he ate? Do you really think a caterpillar would eat all these foods? Why or why not? How do you think the caterpillar would feel? How do you feel when you eat too much?

- After the story, ask children if they thought the caterpillar would turn into a butterfly? Use this story to talk briefly about life cycles—always the same steps in the cycle.

After the story, share or demonstrate possible extension activities that can enrich the storytime experience. Display nonfiction books. Mention a few nonfiction books about caterpillars and other insects to help participants see the many possibilities of extending discussion beyond the original storytime book. Show or suggest simple caterpillar craft activities as extensions involving the arts, fine motor development, and fun.

Talking Points: Share or Demonstrate Extension Activities

- To enrich the storytime experience, you may want to catch a caterpillar to showcase in a jar. Or if the season and location are appropriate, take a walk to see if you can find a caterpillar. There are also online sources to buy a pupa that the children can watch hatch to see the butterfly that emerges after the caterpillar eats its food and makes the pupa.

- Are there other stories about caterpillars or insects you might think of to create a theme for a week or month?

Trainer Peg Pond and interpreter Martha Portocarrero present the activity card and instructions for The Very Hungry Caterpillar activity at a workshop for Spanish-speaking parents.

Talking Points: Review Storytime Techniques Using The Very Hungry Caterpillar *Chart*

- [Refer to PowerPoint or large, readable chart *(see appendix E, web extra 18)* posted in the room to review the techniques and strategies you used in sharing the story and their significance to the experience and development of school readiness and reading skills. Provide a binder-size copy of your completed sample chart for them to take home and refer back to as they do their future planning.]

- You should always preview stories you will be sharing to ensure that you are comfortable with the content, age appropriateness, and the like. Also, check to see if there are words you think the children might not understand. Decide whether to introduce the new vocabulary before, during, or after reading the story.

- The pretend caterpillar play at the beginning of the story sharing gains the children's attention, introduces the story's character, engages children by tying into pretend play, fosters their imaginations, and uses actions and repetition to teach directional words and concepts such as *behind, over, on top of.*

- Introducing the book by looking at and talking about the cover and sharing the information on the cover builds print awareness and prereading skills. Here you are helping children understand about titles, authors, and illustrators. It is important to use the correct terms even though they may be difficult for children to say or totally understand at first. This is an ongoing learning process that is reinforced over time. Together, authors and illustrators make the book. Additionally, by pointing to the words of the title as you read, children begin to understand that the squiggles are words that you are reading left to right, and top to bottom.

- Asking questions about children's experiences or what they think will happen in the story draws on "me"-centered learning and increases their thinking and reasoning process.

- Children's imagination should be encouraged, not stifled. You may be blessed with many bizarre and "out there" answers to predicting questions you ask as you read stories. For these early years, birth to five, there are really no right or wrong answers to the questions—they are their predictions—what they've thought of in answer to your question. With preschoolers especially, it is important to try to help them understand how or why they came up with the answer they give: "Why do you think the caterpillar will feel good after eating all those foods?" *There are no right or wrong answers—it is the process of imagination and problem solving that counts.*

- Using pacing, varied inflection, and a variety of voices helps make the story come alive, holds the attention of the audience, and brings fun to the activity.

- When asking predicting questions or talking about illustrations during the story, be careful not to interrupt the flow of the story too often. If you disrupt the flow too often, children lose track of the story, become bored, and you lose them before the end. "Children learn most from books when they are actively involved" is a premise of dialogic reading, a book-sharing technique developed by the Stony Brook Reading and Language Project. You can find out more about this technique from the Reading Rockets website. We did not specifically follow this book-sharing model, but the premise of the techniques we modeled is the same: involve the children in the story as you read to them.

- Asking the children to help you count the fruit keeps them engaged and builds mathematical skills.

- Pointing out vocabulary words that may be new to the children, then defining and talking about them, are critical parts of building vocabulary and language skills. You help children understand a new concept so that later they can use the word in context themselves. This is an ongoing, repetitive learning process.

- Using the physical motions of rubbing their tummies when they are too full demonstrates how children have fun while relating the experience of the caterpillar to themselves. Learning is "me"-centered.

- Talking about the surprise butterfly at the end and the sequence of the story helps children learn that stories have an order—beginning, middle, and end—and introduces the scientific concept of life cycles.

B. *Hands-on Activity Using Kit Books to Develop Techniques for Sharing the Story and Extension Activities*

For the activity, provide an assortment of picture books (from the take-home kit). Have participants select one for their table and work together as a group to brainstorm and chart how to extend the story in a similar manner. Provide blank paper for writing brainstorming ideas and a blank copy of the chart used for *The Very Hungry Caterpillar* (web extra 19). The chart is divided into three columns with a place for the book title at the top. Provide the following headings for the three columns: Read-Aloud, Extension Activities, and Children Learn. Typically we allow 10–15 minutes for this activity.

Talking Points

- At each of your tables, will one person volunteer to write down your ideas on the blank piece(s) of paper? Together as a group quickly read and look through the picture book.

- First, brainstorm ideas for ways to share the book, like in the first column for *The Very Hungry Caterpillar* chart. Brainstorming simply means sharing ideas as they come to you—no discussion, no right or wrong, just get ideas out there to think about.

- Second, brainstorm ideas for possible extension activities for follow-up after the story, as in the second column on *The Very Hungry Caterpillar* chart. You do not have to come up with domains of learning that will be taking place by using the activities; it is more important at this time to think of the additional activities themselves.

- Finally, discuss ideas recorded in the two brainstorming sections and have the recorder put the ones your group chooses in the correct column on your blank chart. For example, in column one you may have "Point to words in the title as you read the title" as one of your techniques. For the Extension Activities column you may choose "Retell the story with a flannelboard" as your extension. You should have a list of several ideas for each column.

- Do you have any questions? You have __ minutes to work on this activity.

Participants discuss extension activities for the book Chicka Chicka Boom Boom.

- [After the allotted time] Each table please report out by sharing your book title and one or two ideas for the first and second columns of the chart.

- Please don't repeat ideas already expressed by another group.

After the allotted time, you will be facilitating the group sharing. This is a great opportunity to praise the participants' grasp of the story-sharing techniques and their creative ideas for extensions. You may have to guide them gently if they confuse activities with techniques.

C. *Demonstrating Other Ways to Enhance a Story: Fingerplay Glove Activity*

Demonstrate other interactive and fun ways to enhance story sharing and extension activities using resources such as puppets, lap theater, flannelboard, and a fingerplay glove.

Fingerplay glove

We selected a bear-themed glove as a "make-it, take-it" extension activity for *Goldilocks and the Three Bears* by Jan Brett. Provide all supplies needed at each table. Be sure you include sufficient scissors, tacky glue, and materials for each table so time is not lost as participants wait for supplies to work on their glove or project. Ideally participants will complete the activity in the allotted time. If they do not finish, provide bags for them to take the parts with them (*see appendix F, web extra 20,* for a sample fingerplay).

Talking Points

- Fingerplay gloves are a great interactive extension activity for stories. Use them to introduce stories or themes, or just have fun with them. Using the glove while saying the rhyme with the children helps build confidence as they learn the rhyme.

- Explore concepts and skills, including counting, colors, seasons, and phonological awareness, through fingerplay rhymes.

- Because fingerplay rhymes involve adding or taking away from the number of objects on the fingers, practice putting on the glove first to see which way to face your hand so it is easiest for you to fold down your fingers as you say the rhyme. This determines which side of the glove you attach your bears or other objects to. [Demonstrate this with your sample glove by having the participants repeat a bear fingerplay with you, using their bare fingers as if they had a glove on to fold down as you count down in the rhyme. Repeat the rhyme twice so they have an opportunity to determine what is most comfortable for them.]

- Be creative. For example, the bear heads on your glove do not have to be realistic. Children enjoy them as much or more if they are colorful and silly.

VI. Kindergarten Skills Matching Activity (25 minutes total)

A component of our training program is sharing information with participants about the schools' expectations for children entering kindergarten. We used the indicators for the language and literacy domain from the Pearson Work Sampling System for our activity. Since this is a widely used early learning assessment tool across the country, the indicators are likely to dovetail with your state's expectations (*see appendix G, web extra 21,* for a set of the indicators and snapshot sets of behaviors of children beginning to develop an understanding of these indicators).

Duplicate the indicators on colored card stock. Duplicate the behaviors that show children are beginning to grasp the indicators on white card stock. Distribute sets to each table and provide an answer key to tables to self-check their responses as they work at matching the indicators and behaviors. Review a sample of an indicator and a behavior before the participants begin. Take a few minutes to debrief after the activity and answer any questions. Ask participants to share if they have seen their children display any of these behaviors. The behaviors represent a range of development that occurs between the ages of two and five.

Talking Points

- This activity is based upon the Pearson Work Sampling System, an early childhood assessment program used in Maryland and in many other states across the country. According to Pearson, it "provides observational assessment to systematically document children's skills, knowledge, behavior, and academic accomplishments in seven domains."

- We will be using indicators and behaviors from the language and literacy domain.

- The indicators are in color and the descriptions of behaviors of young children are in white. [Use your chosen example to demonstrate matching behaviors with an indicator.] The behaviors listed are those children begin to display as they gain an understanding of those indicators.

- Work together to match the indicators and the children's behaviors. There are three behaviors for each indicator.

- Many of the areas can overlap, so it can be tricky to match behaviors. This activity helps you gain a feel for the kindergarten expectations. The importance of the activity is to help you gain an understanding of how your children will demonstrate their developing skills in the key areas of early literacy.

- After completing your matching, use the answer key so you can self-check your responses.

VIIa.   **[Child Care Professional Workshop] Parental Involvement Introduction/ Activity (10 minutes total)**

Presenting a parental involvement activity can motivate professionals to inform and mentor parents to be involved in their child's learning. After giving a few examples, conduct a brainstorming session. Use chart paper for recording and encourage providers to take notes of any new ideas from their colleagues they might like to try.

Talking Points

- It is important to involve parents in the learning process.
- Tell your children's parents that you have a school readiness curriculum that uses research-based principles. Explain that you take training workshops each year, such as today's training, that teach these principles. You can frame and display your certificates for parents to see.
- Tell parents that they need to reinforce your learning activities at home. Remind them that they have an important role as their child's first teacher.
- You can educate parents about school readiness and encourage them to reinforce these skills at home. For example:

Tell them that it is easy to use books to introduce concepts, such as teaching the concepts *small, medium,* and *large* using the storybook *Goldilocks and the Three Bears* by Jan Brett.

Suggest that they can help reinforce the concept of purposeful reading (reading for performing a specific task). For example, when making a recipe in the kitchen, they can say to their child, "I'm going to bake a cake, let's read the recipe." Or when assembling a new toy with their child, they can say, "Let's read the directions on how to put this toy together."

Type a school readiness tip on a slip of paper or include it in a newsletter to send home with the parents. [Sample tips are available in web extra 22.]

You can use the following samples from our workshop to supplement your participants' discussion, if needed.

Share videos or photos of children' activities, especially during holidays, such as making a card for Valentine's Day, Mother's Day, or Father's Day or making a Christmas ornament.

Send samples of child's work home for parents to see. Include a note explaining the school readiness skills learned.

Send assignments home occasionally; for example, an activity a child needs to complete and bring back to child care, such as a family picture to share when talking about families; or an object the child should bring back to child care, like a pair of old shoes for taking a special nature walk or a favorite stuffed animal to go with a storytime extension activity.

Send back homework for parents—activities for them to do at home with their children.

VIIb. [Parent Workshop] Show-and-Tell of Remaining Materials in Kit (10 minutes total)

Parents may not be as familiar with early childhood development as many child care providers. Share more items in the take-home kit along with ways they can be used with children. If there is not a take-home kit, provide examples and demonstrate ways to develop skills using items they may have in their home. Samples of school readiness skills and activities as talking points are available as web extra 23.

Have extras of some materials that can be shared at each table by the participants during this show-and-tell/group activity portion of the workshop. Although we provided Ready At Five materials, we encouraged parents' creativity in thinking of other ways they can use the items, for example, using colored construction paper for drawing or making a book, or placing sheets on the floor for a bean bag toss to match colors. Show them samples of what they can do at home to highlight a specific skill. If you were highlighting how to teach shapes and patterns, you may, for example (a) use construction paper to draw shapes and patterns, (b) create a chart with samples of patterns using colors, shapes, stickers, (c) cut out pictures for children to trace shapes, such as a house or boat, or (d) use patterned cloth to show patterns in our everyday settings.

After demonstrating a variety of activities, have participants work together to come up with ways they could use the items to play with their children.

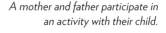

A mother and father participate in an activity with their child.

Talking Points

- Skills your children will need to be successful in kindergarten can be developed using simple materials to make these learning experiences fun during parent/child time together.

- Many things you have in your home, such as egg cartons, paper, balls, measuring cups and spoons, spaghetti, and yarn, can be used to enjoy learning activities with children. Other inexpensive resources may be found at a discount store or Goodwill.

VIII.   Music and Movement (10 minutes total)

Have some method of sharing music CDs or songs—a CD player or iPod with speakers, for example. To present this section effectively, have your children's songs ready to be played in the order you will be introducing them and related activities. Before introducing this section, hand out activity items—scarves, streamers, bubbles, a ball, beanbags— that participants will be using for movement during the songs. You will not have time to play entire songs, just enough to give them a flavor of the activity.

Talking Points

- Remember the 3 Rs, Rhythm, Rhyme, and Repetition? They are critical for brain development, especially prereading skills.

- Music is an excellent learning tool that encompasses all three learning strategies. Through repetition and rhyme in songs, the brain is strengthening important neural memory connections. The rhythms of different kinds of music—whether jazz, classical, rock, or country—help build patterns in the brain that promote speech and language.

- Our brains build stronger memory connections when learning is put to music or rhythms.

- Nursery rhyme songs have survived for centuries as a way of helping children learn while having fun with rhythm. The creators of television commercials understand the power of music, which is why many use catchy jingles. We often remember them for years, like "free credit report dot com" or Coke's "I'd like to teach the world to sing" music commercials. Many of us learned the letters of the alphabet by singing the alphabet song.

- Using props with music enhances the fun and fosters skill development across all learning domains, especially language and literacy.

- One activity that is fun for all ages is using bubbles with music. "Bubbles" by Parachute Express or any peppy song/instrumental would suffice. With the youngest children you can make the bubbles during the song as very young children move and dance. Older preschool children enjoy making their own bubbles during the song. [Play your song. Have everyone join in using bubbles.]

- [Participants may be reluctant to "let their hair down" or get into the music and movement activity at first. *Remind them that they should enjoy being children during this part of the workshop.* Demonstrate your enthusiasm with movement while encouraging them to let themselves go and have fun.]

- You can use silly songs such as "Down by the Bay." Music can reinforce a sense of fun while building rhyming, rhythm, and concept skills.

- You may use a simple object, such as a ball, to build concept skills while having fun with instrumental music.

- [Play your next song and have participants pass an object to the music and give them instructions, such as passing it behind themselves, over their head, to the left, to the right, modeling how they can do this with their children.] By giving instructions during a song you are supporting listening skills, following directions, and learning spatial concepts.

- There are many wonderful songs that don't need props, only your body, such as "The Hokey Pokey," "Silly Dance Contest" by Jim Gill, "Whenever I Hear the Music" by the Wiggles, or "Put Your Finger On" by Parachute Express.

- [Play your next song using scarves or streamers.] Children enjoy the movement, color, and fun of using scarves or streamers to enhance the music experience. This develops not only small and large motor control but also following directions and rules for safety, such as standing far enough away from others to move freely and being careful of movements during the song.

- Using music with children in any way is a win-win situation for you and for them as learning and fun go together.

IX. Workshop Wrap-Up (10 minutes total)

Have each participant complete a workshop evaluation form or quick-write evaluation. With a quick-write evaluation, participants simply write their immediate overall impressions for the workshop, using a couple of guiding questions. Give each participant a whole or half sheet of blank paper. To encourage participants to give accurate feedback, keep responses anonymous. Take a few moments to have participants complete the evaluation.

Talking Points

- Please take a few minutes to give us feedback. We're passing out a half sheet of blank paper. We would just like you to share with us some of your most important thoughts or impressions of today's workshop. Here are a few questions to think about to provide useful information to us:

    What worked well?

    What could have been done differently to be more effective?

    What would you like to know more about?

    What one idea or insight will you immediately use when you go back to your child care setting?

    Was there reinforcement in today's workshop of what you are already doing?

- Thank you! This feedback is important in helping the library with future workshops.

- [For Child Care Professionals] Your certificates will be given out at the end of the spring workshop.

- We have provided you with many ideas and resources today, and we hope you are as excited as we are about the possibilities. Please don't be afraid to experiment and have fun. We know your children will learn in the process.

- Remember, it is not important that you do each activity perfectly, but that you explore the resources and observe your children's growing understanding of the concepts. Encourage your children to be curious. Follow up and expand on their interests.

- You will receive a phone call in the next couple of months. We will ask you to talk about the books and materials you are trying and how the children are responding. One or two of your comments will be included in an upcoming newsletter. Please save some of the children's samples and take some notes about key observations you would like to share at the spring training.

- We can't wait to hear about your adventures and see examples in the spring.

- Keep the date open for the spring follow-up training. There will be some new materials and ideas, but the follow-up workshop will mainly be your opportunity to share and discuss the wonderful things you have been doing with the fall workshop materials. It will be an opportunity to celebrate your accomplishments and to learn from one another.

- Thank you for your time and participation today. You have all contributed to the learning happening today for your children's future success in school.

POINTS TO PONDER

☐ Will you use a pre-survey to assess the background knowledge of your audience? If so, when will you have participants complete it so that the information is most useful to you? Are there other ways you can help identify the knowledge level of your audience; for example, do you have bookmobile or early literacy van service to child care professionals where library staff already have a relationship?

☐ Do you have community partners who have relationships with parents?

☐ Do you remember to engage and inspire all levels of learners when you conduct training?

☐ Do you know how pretend or dramatic play can help children develop self-regulation, motivation, and curiosity?

☐ Which parts of the workshop do you need to rehearse more? Do you have any colleagues with expertise in these areas who could assist you in your preparation?

Ongoing Support and Celebration

After the primary workshop, you can offer support and a follow-up workshop that is not time consuming on your part. A goal of part 3 of this book is to offer guidelines that motivate participants to "see it, do it, and teach it." You want them to return for the follow-up workshop having tried the materials and activities and having observed changes in their children's skill levels. You want them to be excited to share and discuss with colleagues.

> *Correction does much, but encouragement does more.*
> —JOHANN WOLFGANG VON GOETHE

Ongoing Support

One of the keys to our program's success was the support provided between the fall and spring workshops. Bimonthly newsletters allowed us to provide additional information, tips, and encouragement (*see appendix H, web extras 24 and 25*). With each newsletter, we sent an additional resource: puppets, CDs, something to keep motivation high. Phone calls allowed participants to discuss how the program was going and gave them the opportunity to share their success stories in an upcoming newsletter. Participant questions could also be answered during the calls. These components were an integral part of the program design.

During the initial training, participants were informed that there would be follow-up by phone or online. We suggest making contact twice before the follow-up training.

The following questions will be useful to guide these conversations with providers:

- How are things going?

- What one or two activities have you applied that worked well?

- Have you noticed growth in the children's early literacy skills in any particular area?

- Are the children enjoying the activities, and do they seem to be motivated to learn?

- Have you or the children come up with any extensions or related activities to the resources provided? If so, please share a couple.

- Were there activities that did not work well? Why do you think that is so?

- Have you tried using tips from the reading ring? What have been the children's reactions to being included in using the reading ring to decide on follow-up activities?

- Have you tried any other parent involvement activities? Have you had a chance to share any information with parents to encourage their involvement with their child's developing skills or the activities you are doing in your child care setting?

- Do you have any feedback about the materials in the kit? Have you used the handouts from the workshop?

The Follow-up Workshop and Celebration

Your participants will be excited to come back together and share their experiences if you provide this ongoing support. We suggest making the follow-up workshop a celebration to encourage ongoing camaraderie, peer coaching, and creativity. This workshop's priorities are to share and celebrate what is working, provide new information and resources, and discuss how to refine and extend application of skills and techniques. It is also important to motivate participants to continue using their training and invite them to stay in touch with you and the library.

A suggested agenda for the follow-up workshop is in appendix I. Some details are as follows:

I. Welcome/Housekeeping/Collect Survey (5 minutes)

II. Review Training Program Goals (10 minutes)

III. Sharing Session (50 minutes)

This provider and her child care children were inspired to create a puppet theater after receiving puppets as a resource.

This session is an empowering opportunity for participants to share their own and each other's successes. This is also an important opportunity for the trainers to provide sincere verbal praise and to acknowledge the workshop attendees' active participation in the program and their creative, enthusiastic interactions with their children. Have one presenter write discussion comments on a flip chart. Capture participant responses for each of the books, materials, and activities they share, including ages of children, responses by the children to the books or activities, and any other extension activities they created. Appendix J offers a few examples of the comments we received.

Talking Points

- We acknowledge your caring, creativity, and follow-through in using your new skills. We recognize the challenges you face and admire your dedication in providing learning opportunities for your children.

- Please continue to seek out ways to support and reinforce each other. Peer coaching is an ideal way for ongoing support and growth.

- Now let's start the fun and excitement of sharing your experiences and the samples you brought to share.

IV. **Snapshots of Early Literacy Development (15 minutes)**

We developed a set of informal assessment tools to share at the follow-up workshop. We called these tools "Snapshots of Early Literacy Development," and we created one for each of the key areas covered in the training package (*below, and web extras 26–29*). The goal is to have participants use these tools when observing skill development in their children.

CONCEPTS ABOUT PRINT: WHAT ARE YOU SEEING?

- ☐ Can the children recognize their favorite books by the covers?
- ☐ Can the children identify the front and back covers of a book?
- ☐ Are the children able to point to the title of a favorite book?
- ☐ Do the children understand that the print is what you are reading?
- ☐ Are the children beginning to understand that print tracks from left to right and top to bottom?

PHONOLOGICAL AWARENESS: WHAT ARE YOU SEEING?

- ☐ Are the children chiming in more consistently when you share rhyming stories, poems, and songs?
- ☐ Can the children tell you if two words rhyme or not when you say them?
- ☐ Can the children make up their own rhymes?
- ☐ Can the children clap syllables in two-syllable words?
- ☐ If you give the children a sound to listen for (e.g., /t/), and then say three words (e.g., *turtle, tub, soup*), can they tell you the words that start with /t/?

ALPHABETIC PRINCIPLE: WHAT ARE YOU SEEING?

- ☐ Can the children recognize and identify some or all of the letters in their first name?

- ☐ How many upper- and lowercase letters can the children recognize and name? Do you feel they are making progress from the fall?

- ☐ Are the children showing interest in learning how to write their names?

- ☐ Are the children connecting any of the letters to the sounds they make?

- ☐ Are any of the children showing interest in writing on their own?

- ☐ Do the children understand the concept of a word yet?

COMPREHENSION AND ORAL LANGUAGE: WHAT ARE YOU SEEING?

- ☐ Can the children make a logical prediction about what a book will be about when you read the title and talk about the cover picture together?

- ☐ Can the children make logical predictions during reading when you stop and ask them "What do think will happen next?"

- ☐ Are the children picking up on new vocabulary from the books you share or the conversations you have together?

- ☐ Can the children retell parts of the story when you share a book, particularly a favorite one? Can anyone retell the whole story by telling you something that happened in the beginning, the middle, and the end?

- ☐ Are the children starting to make connections to the story by telling you how a character or event relates to their own experiences?

- ☐ Are the children more verbal, in general, than they were in the fall?

In the workshop, present the four Snapshot documents with the participants. Assign one of the four documents to each table and have participants discuss what they have observed in their children so far for each of the questions. Provide copies of all Snapshots for each participant to keep.

Talking Points

- You are continuously taking "snapshots" of your children's progress as you observe their daily behavior during playtime and structured learning activities.

- You can see how these questions parallel skills and strategies you have been reinforcing.

- Do you remember the matching activity you did in the initial workshop—where you matched the kindergarten indicators to the behaviors children exhibit as they are developing these skills. The Snapshots represent the same concept: you are trying to see where the children are on their way to developing school readiness skills in these key areas.

V. Promoting Print Awareness and the Enjoyment of Reading (25 minutes)

At this point in the workshop, we promoted new ideas to encourage print awareness and the enjoyment of sharing books together. Have examples of environmental print—words from food boxes, advertisements, magazines—available to show and to explain how pointing out print in the children's world helps them understand that print has meaning. Provide samples and demonstrate techniques for bookmaking ideas you share, such as using book jackets you provide as a starting point to create their own book, fold-a-book, or flipbooks. Have them begin to make their own fold-a-book or other homemade book using a concept or theme you choose, such as a counting book. Have available at each table appropriate supplies.

Talking Points

- Environmental print can be used to develop prereading skills and harness an interest in learning letters and reading. Environmental print is simply the words that children see every day throughout their environment, including restaurant signs, food boxes, store names, and road signs, to name a few.

- Even the youngest children become familiar with things such as their favorite cereal box. You can use this packaging to help them learn the letters that make up the words, like Cheerios and Kraft. To make learning fun, you can create games using names and words from boxes, cans, or magazines. Spread them on a table and ask them to find a specific letter as quickly as they can. Provide environmental words in a play area also.

- Children have fun and are engaged in learning when they have the opportunity to make their own books.

- The books can be about letters, numbers, concepts, or things they like.

- The books can be small and simple, such as a fold-a-book.

- Resources for making their own books are simple and inexpensive: colored paper or lined paper, markers, crayons, pencils, magazine pictures, and so forth.

- Creating their own story for a picture book is fun, encourages imagination, promotes self-esteem and confidence, assists with learning the parts of a book, and builds skills for working together in a group.

The children can begin with the picture on the book jacket (or maybe from a magazine if book jackets aren't available) as a jumping-off point for using their imagination to decide what they want their book to be about and what their title will be. Help them write the title on the front cover of their book with the book jacket picture.

The children can develop the story as you help them write down what they decide. Then they can each be given a page or pages of the story to draw a picture to go with their story as you have written it down.

· [For child care providers] Sharing the results with parents contributes to their understanding of the learning taking place in your child care setting; builds pride and reinforces the children's learning skills through their success; and, we hope, encourages parents to engage in reading activities with their child at home.

A great closing activity is to share or "book-talk" some of your favorite and new picture books. Have various book lists to distribute, with suggested books to use with children. You may have lists of theme-related, age-appropriate books (e.g., on feelings, baby animals, holidays), book lists based on age categories, or lists from your workshop booktalks.

Participants in the follow-up workshop

VI. Evaluation and Closing (15 minutes)

To wrap up your workshop, focus on additional ways you might help participants celebrate their efforts and successes. Some possibilities to be considered:

· Cake or special "party" refreshments

· Additional educational resource, perhaps a useful professional book such as one with storytime themes and patterns, an educational game, or other support for learning

· Personal thank-you note to each participant for their participation, with a bookmark or small container of candy

· Certificate of completion or participation (*see web extra 30*)

· Verbally thank participants for their time and outstanding response to your program

· Encourage them to contact each other for ongoing peer coaching and feedback

· Encourage them to keep learning and have fun with their children

We recommend using a prepared written evaluation along with the post-survey to assist you in assessing the progress and results of your project. Using a written evaluation about the training and a post-survey reflecting what participants learned gives you valuable input to guide your future initiatives.

The feedback you collect from workshop discussions and surveys, along with phone and online correspondence, can be transformed into advocacy information for public officials, administrators, and other decision makers. Additionally, statistics can be gathered from your workshop notes, discussion notes, surveys, and evaluations to help you with reports required by funders and for future funding.

Training Team Final Assessment Meeting

Take a deep breath and congratulate yourselves on completing your project. Now it is time to celebrate your successes and to evaluate the program. Always remember, no project is ever perfect and can always benefit from tweaking or changes, especially after the first time it is completed. As soon as feasible, once you have gathered all your information about the project—surveys, evaluations, notes during workshops, feedback from participants, financial reports, and anything else that is relevant—schedule a trainers' meeting.

Set your agenda to review your data, analyze what worked well; what didn't, if anything; what changes the team might recommend, if any; what problems arose; and whether those problems were adequately addressed. Then consider ways to celebrate and reward your training team. It is important to acknowledge you and your team's achievements, creativity, dedication, and success.

Remember to recognize your partners and your volunteers in some way. Now relax, until you're ready to gear up for the next presentation.

POINTS TO **PONDER**

☐ Have you thought of the impact of ongoing support to your training program?

☐ Do you have techniques for encouraging sharing of successful practices that you could use to facilitate the participants' sharing session?

☐ Do you have examples of bookmaking activities for preschoolers that you could use?

☐ Have you thought through how to provide a festive, celebratory atmosphere for the follow-up workshop?

CHAPTER 10

Using Best Practices to Customize Your Training Package

The tools in this chapter are summaries to help you invoke your ideal vision and to show you how to use this book to plan and create a realistic training package that fits your library staffing, funding, and community needs.

Questions to Invoke Your Ideal Training Vision

By taking a few minutes to invoke your ideal vision, you can lay a strong foundation to build on during the weeks and months ahead as you create your training program. Ask yourself these questions:

1. Have you noticed that you are more open to new ideas or to trying something different when you are relaxed and having fun? What would a best-case scenario look like in your workshop where participants are receptive and engaged? *(chapter 1)*

> *Nothing great was ever achieved without enthusiasm.*
> —RALPH WALDO EMERSON

SAMPLES OF KEY AUDIENCES

☐ Family home child providers

☐ Child care center staff

☐ A mix of home providers and center staff

☐ Early childhood educators, such as preschool and Head Start teachers

☐ Parents and other caregivers—with no socioeconomic restrictions

☐ Parents and other caregivers based on at-risk socioeconomic criteria

☐ Parents and other caregivers who are English language learners

2. In a perfect world, how would you connect community partners to your training efforts? What role would partners play: promote training? recruit participants? donate materials or funds? *(chapter 2)*

SAMPLE OF COMMUNITY PARTNERS

☐ School system

☐ Early Childhood coalition

☐ Child care association

☐ Head Start

☐ Businesses

☐ Churches

3. Do you understand the basic research about the economic and educational aspects of reaching children in their early years? Pick one or two sources from the list of resources at the end of the book to help you reach a new understanding.

4. How do Carroll County Public Library's research results *(see chapter 3)* influence your thinking about responding to the needs of children and caregivers in developing school readiness skills in your community? What are your ideal results you would like to achieve?

5. What is your learning philosophy? *(chapter 4)* Specifically, what would you do to apply a learning philosophy to your workshop in order for participants to be more motivated and capable of assessing their own knowledge, skills, and growth? *(chapter 8)*

You are responsible for your own learning!

Tap the power of the "see it, do it, teach it" approach.

6. Do you see the value of moving beyond one-shot workshops to a structure of continued opportunities for participants to learn and grow together? What kind of opportunities might you implement? *(chapter 4)*

OPPORTUNITIES FOR CONTINUED CONTACT

☐ Newsletters sharing additional tips and including comments from workshop participants about the new skills/techniques they are using

☐ Online blogs or discussion boards

☐ Phone conversations

☐ Follow-up workshops to share and celebrate what is working, provide new information, and discuss how to refine and extend application of skills and techniques

7. Can you picture participants having ah-ha moments in your workshop and applying the training in their daily activities? *(chapter 5)*

8. How might participants become more willing to learn new things? *(chapter 6)*

9. What is the optimal time frame for your training program? *(chapter 7)*

10. Can you envision the possibilities for making an impact in your community? *(chapter 7)*

THE TRAINING PROGRAM WILL

☐ Encourage caregivers and engage parents to be involved in the child's learning

☐ Focus on conversation, book sharing, and play to develop school readiness skills

☐ Use everyday materials, books, and hands-on activities

☐ Be fun!

11. How might you engage and inspire all levels of learners? *(chapter 8)*

12. In a perfect world, what are the ways you would like to provide ongoing support/contact? *(chapter 9)*

Our Conclusions in a Nutshell

The components of the training program that we believe make the biggest difference in fostering school readiness:

· An initial workshop of four hours for child care professionals and two hours for parents with a homework assignment to do activities

Each person can strive to become a lifelong learner by consistently evaluating what worked well and what could have been done differently in a situation to produce better results.

It is important to demonstrate respect and set the right tone by communicating in a friendly yet businesslike manner.

- A take-home kit of books and resources
- Ongoing support in the form of an occasional phone call or e-mail message and newsletters
- A follow-up two-hour workshop with time to share and discuss children's growth
- A learning philosophy that emphasizes that we are each responsible for our own learning and use a "see it, do it, teach it" approach
- Transfer of learning by encouraging activities between the workshops and beyond the training program
- Encouragement of peer feedback and coaching
- Hands-on activities
- Great content that uses research-based practices
- Bringing out the participants' best at whatever level they are starting

Quick Checklist for Early Literacy and School Readiness Training

- Do you have a clear and concise proposal/pitch for administration and community buy-in—one that cites research-based results, includes a realistic time line, and can be presented in five minutes or less? *(chapter 7)*
- Do you have a prepared budget projection—one that is realistic for your library and community? *(chapter 7)*

BUDGET GUIDELINES

Supplying a kit of ready-to-use materials along with ongoing staff support can increase a participant's transfer of learning. An ideal budget scenario might include

- ☐ Cost for books and materials using the Ready At Five activity cards, **$100–$200 per kit**
- ☐ Cost for light refreshments, **$2–$3 per person**
- ☐ Cost for additional resources (books, professional resources, play materials) to be distributed with the newsletters and at a follow-up workshop, **$25–$75 per person**
- ☐ Cost of startup workshop supplies, such as flip chart paper, markers, and sticky notes, **$15–$75**

- Do you plan to seek outside funding—grants, sponsors, or partnerships? If so, have you included this task in your time line? *(chapter 7)*
- Are community partners included in your planning as a way to develop and support your training program, such as with letters of support for

grants and other funding, by lending their staff and volunteers to assist or providing books and materials, as well as giving monetary support? *(chapter 7)*

· Does your plan include program logistics specific to your training program needs—such as who will present the training, location for the workshops, funding, training supplies, refreshments, confirmation letters/calls, room setup? *(chapter 7)*

· Do you have talking points prepared to explain the training program goals when you recruit participants? *(chapter 7)*

· Do you have a plan to find out what your participants know—before the training to gauge their knowledge level to help you prepare the training—and afterward to gauge what participants learned? *(chapter 7)*

· Do you have a prepared and enthusiastic trainer or training team? *(chapter 7)*

· Will you provide a school readiness kit? Is it ready? *(chapter 7)*

· Have you prepared your initial workshop presentation in a way that the learners ponder what the information means to them and how it applies to their specific situation? *(chapter 8)*

· Are you providing engaging hands-on experiences in the initial workshop to encourage the use of modeled behaviors? *(chapter 8)*

· Are you providing opportunities for group brainstorming, discussion, and interaction during the workshops? *(chapter 8)*

· Are you encouraging peer coaching and feedback techniques to increase the transfer of learning into daily activities? *(chapter 8)*

· Will you provide a follow-up workshop? *(chapter 9)*

· Either way, do you have a plan for ongoing support after the primary workshop, such as occasional online or phone contact and newsletters to help sustain enthusiasm and interest to use the books, materials, and activities—and to encourage peer coaching/feedback?

· Will you collect and use testimonials and success stories to market the training in the future and for your administration to use with public officials? *(chapter 9)*

· Do you and your team have a method for reflecting and learning from the process? *(chapter 9)*

Our motto is, be relentlessly proactive and cheerful!.

Thomas, who was with Ms. Katie for a whole year, is now five, and it is his first day of kindergarten. He is eager to go to school and happily says good-bye to his mom at the door. Thomas recognizes his name right away on his kindergarten storage cubby and feels right at home. He likes the look of activity centers and books around the room. Thomas decides to first try the building block area. He easily makes new friends with a few classmates who are in the same area. They begin to work together on building a bridge and a wall across the whole space. Throughout the day, he easily follows the teacher's direction when it is time to end one activity and begin another. Thomas is proud that he is allowed to help clean up the play areas before they begin sharing. He is able to tell the teacher and his classmates about his family—his mother, father, and big sister—when the teacher asks the children to share so that they get to know each other. During reading time, he listens attentively to the story the teacher reads, *The Very Hungry Caterpillar,* and eagerly raises his hand to answer predicting questions about the caterpillar. The teacher asks if anyone has heard about the life cycle. Thomas again raises his hand to answer the question, saying, "Caterpillar to butterfly, caterpillar to butterfly!" He relishes the movement time when the class has fun marching to a song. He waits quietly in line and uses his manners during lunch. Later in the afternoon, when the children draw pictures about their favorite part of the story, Thomas draws a triumphant butterfly and proudly prints his name on his paper. His teacher is thrilled to note his confidence and enthusiasm for learning on the first day of school.

Always walk through life as if you have something new to learn and you will.
—VERNON HOWARD

Public libraries have the opportunity and the potential to become increasingly relevant in the twenty-first century. This cannot be just a haphazard stab in the dark. It is important to conduct research on the value of library programs and services. It is important to give thoughtful attention to results, whether you are conducting formal research or informally determining your impact. Each library is responsible for finding what tools work well. Which programs and services are working? What can libraries do differently to become more effective? Who can help you measure your impact—universities? other research organizations? What formal and informal methods of evaluation will prove useful? Do you listen to anecdotes and feedback from library customers?

These types of questions can lead you, as they did Carroll County Public Library, to a profound understanding of what the library needs to do to redefine itself.

In May 2011, Pierce County (Washington) Public Library, working with the University of Washington, reported positive results from a training program and research study similar to the Carroll County project:

> It is encouraging that there have now been two randomized studies, Carroll County MD and Pierce County WA, in which statistically significant results occurred for three of the four early literacy principles when library training for childcare workers took place. More studies of this type will continue to build confidence in the efficacy of the public library's extended role in preparing children for success in school.[1]

In the area of school readiness, libraries are leading the way to lifelong enjoyment of learning by challenging parents and professionals to inspire young children to learn.

NOTE

1. Eliza T. Dresang and Kathleen Campana, *Emergent Readers Literacy Training and Assessment Program: Research Report* (unpublished report prepared for the Pierce County [WA] Library System), 2011, www.piercecountylibrary.org/files/library/research-report.pdf.

APPENDIX A
Sample Ready At Five Cards

Download or purchase a complete set of cards in seven learning domains from the Ready At Five website, www.readyatfive.org/raf/for-parents/activity-cards.html.

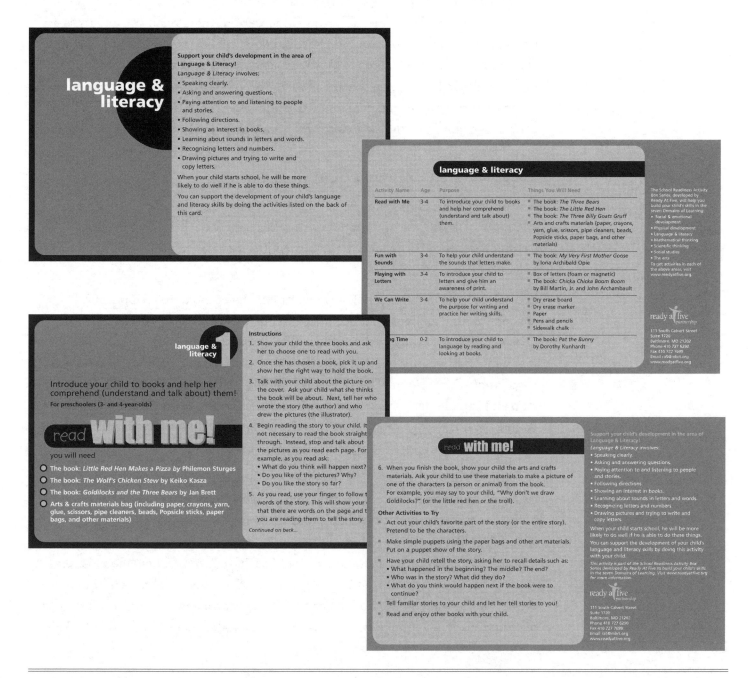

Sample Online Blog Training Entry

Early Literacy and School Readiness Training

This is the workshop presented by Connie Wilson, Elaine Czarnecki, and Dorothy Stoltz. As a follow-up to the workshop, please read this additional information that we hope you will find useful. Please share your thoughts by posting a comment or two.

Comprehension

As we have discussed, comprehension development for young children includes building their oral language. Entering kindergarten with a good vocabulary is a strong predictor of school success. Reading comprehension begins with listening comprehension, and you help to build this when you read and discuss stories together. As children learn to make predictions, retell parts of the story, and relate the story events and characters to their own lives, they are developing the comprehension skills they will need when they learn to read on their own.

Vocabulary and Reading Aloud

A young child's listening and speaking abilities develop ahead of their reading and writing skills. One important way you can help with their oral language development is by increasing their vocabulary when you are reading picture books aloud to them.

You can help your children actively explore the meaning of new words and concepts and give them a chance to use the new words in appropriate context or relationships. For instance, in the book *A Pocket for Corduroy* some words that your children might not recognize or understand are *reluctant, drowsy*, and *desperately*. After you read the sentence in the story that uses each of these words, stop and explain the word by saying something like "Lisa is *reluctant* to leave the Laundromat without Corduroy. *Reluctant* is a word that means you're not sure you want to do something. Let's say that word together—*reluctant*."

At the end of the story, go back and talk about the new words some more to help children understand them in relation to their own lives. Repetition of the sound of the word and the meaning of the word help children add that word to their vocabulary. We all need to hear things more than once to really learn them. For example, with the word *reluctant*, you could ask if they remember when Lisa was reluctant to leave Corduroy at the Laundromat. Ask if they can think of things they might be *reluctant* to do (you can begin by sharing something you would be *reluctant* to do. "I would be *reluctant* to ride on a roller coaster because it looks like it might be scary."). Ask them to use the word when giving you an answer to the question by using the opening phrase "I would be reluctant to . . ." (they might need help with ideas: change my baby sister's diaper, talk to strangers, etc.). If you are using the word *drowsy*, you could ask them to repeat the phrase "I feel drowsy when . . ." and then they add their answer (again, they might need help with ideas: when I stay up too late, when I eat too much, when I've been watching television, etc.). Once they get the idea of the word, they'll probably be able to give you lots of examples or answers using the word.

The four simple steps just described can help children build their vocabulary.

1. Give a *simple, easy-to-understand definition* when reading a new word in a story.

2. Have the children *repeat the word with you.*

3. After the story, help the children *relate the use of the word to something in their own lives.*

4. When they are responding to your question about a situation using the new word that has meaning for them, have them *repeat the word in their answer,* such as, I would be *reluctant* to . . . or I feel *drowsy* when . . .

Early Literacy School Readiness Initial or Primary Workshop Sample Agenda

9:00–9:10:

I. Welcome/introductions/housekeeping; include peer coaching/feedback description. *Librarian*

9:10–9:15:

II. Goals and learning philosophy. *Librarian*

9:15–10:00:

III. School Readiness Information through introduction to resources (handouts/binder/online access), activity cards and take-home kit, hands-on science activity and pretend play activity. *Librarian*

    A. Overview (suggested 5 minutes).

    B. Relate to brain development and social/emotional development (suggested 15 minutes).

    C. Ready At Five Cards* for all domains (domains on wall) and Ready At Five take-home kit contents, including lists of materials and books. Focus on language and literacy domain, but kit is for working in all domains (suggested 5 minutes).

    D. Hands-on activities from science domain (Sink or Float[†] and Science Toolbox) (suggested 10 minutes). *Participants*

    E. Pretend Play skit*[†] and debriefing on what participants observed (suggested 10 minutes). *Librarian*

10:00–10:40:

IV. Early Literacy Development

    A. Review building language skills, comprehension, and learning about letters (suggested 15 minutes). *Librarian*

    B. Phonological awareness (suggested 10 minutes). *Librarian*

    C. Learning about books and print (suggested 10 minutes). *Librarian*

    D. Reading ring[†] (suggested 5 minutes). *Librarian*

10:40–10:55: BREAK

10:55–12:05:

V. Best Practices for sharing books and enhancing learning with extension activities

    A. Model sharing books, talking with children, extension activities (suggested 20 minutes). *Librarian*

    B. Hands-on activity using kit books to develop techniques for sharing the story and extension ideas, then group sharing (suggested 25 minutes). *Participants*

    C. Demonstrating using manipulatives/realia to make learning fun (puppet, flannelboard, lap theater and others) (suggested 10 minutes). *Librarian*

    D. Fingerplay glove activity (suggested 15 minutes). *Participants*

12:05–12:30:

VI. Kindergarten matching activity using examples of skills children will be assessed on in kindergarten.*[†] *Librarian and participants*

12:30–12:40:

VIIa. Involving parents in the learning process (for child care providers). *Librarian and Participants*

    A. Why

    B. How

12:30–12:40:

VIIb. Showing and describing ways to use kit items (for parents). *Librarian*

12:40–12:50:

VIII. Hands-on experience using music for movement, rhyming, language development, fun, etc. *Librarian and participants*

12:50–1:00:

IX. Wrap-up. *Librarian*

    A. Questions (suggested 5 minutes). *Librarian and Participants*

    B. Information about newsletters,*[†] contact calls/emails and spring workshop (suggested 1 minute). *Librarian*

    C. Reminder to do peer coaching/feedback (suggested 1 minute). *Librarian*

    D. Encouragement to have fun, use daily (suggested 1 minute). *Librarian*

    E. Evaluation of workshop[†] (suggested 2 minutes). *Participants*

* Can be found in the appendixes.

[†] Can be found on the ALA Editions Web Extras website, www.alaeditions.org/webextras.

APPENDIX D
Pretend Play Skit Script

The Pretend Play skit demonstrates to adults how they can become a positive part of their child's play. Emphasize to workshop participants that children learn through play and that research shows that when adults are involved in their children's play the children learn more. This skit shows many possible ways for adults to engage children actively in conversation in a play session. In real life adults may want to choose one or two conversation starters instead of several so that the flow of the play is not broken.

Have three copies of your script available for trainers and a volunteer, if necessary. Ask for a volunteer to participate in the skit as needed. Explain why you are including the skit in the workshop.

Pretend Play Script

Connie: Hi, Dorothy and Elaine! I see you are playing doctor. Elaine, is your baby sick?

Elaine: Baby has a cough.

Connie: That's too bad. I'm sure Doctor Dorothy will help your baby feel better. Dorothy, have you been to a doctor's office?

Dorothy: My mother's a nurse.

Connie: Oh, that's wonderful. Did your mother take you to a doctor's office?

Dorothy: Yes, and I got a needle that hurt a lot. I cried.

Connie: I know—I don't like needles either—but doctors and nurses have to use them to give us medicine to make us feel better or to keep us from getting very sick with diseases. Have either of you had to take medicine at home because you had a cough or your ears hurt or maybe your tummy was sick?

Elaine: I had to take red medicine from a spoon, and it tasted good.

Connie: I'm glad it didn't taste yucky and I'm sure it made you feel better. Of course, I know both of you would only take medicine if your mom or dad or other grownup you know gave it to you. It is never safe to take medicine by yourself. That's a good safety rule.
Dorothy, do you know what that is that you have around your neck?

Dorothy: I don't know its name, but the doctor put it on my front at his office.

Connie: That's right, doctors, and sometimes nurses use the stethoscope to listen to your heart and they listen on your chest and your back. It tells them how your heart is working inside. Sometimes it feels cold, but it doesn't hurt. Stethoscope is a big word—can you both say stethoscope?

Elaine and Dorothy: Stethoscope (as a child would try to say it).

Connie: Great! It starts with the s sound—what is the s sound?

Elaine and Dorothy: SSS.

Connie: Right!
Dorothy, do you think you might want to be a doctor some day?

Dorothy: I don't know—I like to play with the doctor stuff, but I don't want to hurt people.

Connie: I know it can seem scary and sometimes it hurts at the doctor's office, but a doctor's job is to help keep you healthy and make you better if you are hurt or sick. Doctors care about you.
Elaine, I see you have a band-aid on your finger—did you get hurt?

Elaine: Yes I cut my finger. Mom made it better—but it did hurt.

Dorothy: Elaine, I don't want to play doctor with you anymore. I want to play alone. Go away!

Elaine: (gets upset) Dorothy, that's mean.

Connie: Dorothy—we've been talking about doctors and making it better when you're hurt. Do you think people only feel hurt when they have a cut or other scrape?

Dorothy: Sometimes you get hurt and break something and have your arm stiff like my brother—that hurt.

Connie: What about getting your feelings hurt? How would you feel if one of your very best friends said, "You're not my best friend anymore. I don't like you. I'm going to play with Janie."?

Dorothy: (Thinks, then says) I would feel bad—I would be very sad. It would feel like mean.

Connie: That's right—sometimes we can say things or do things to other people and make them feel a different kind of hurt—sad and upset inside. These are feelings that we all have and we don't really want to make each other feel that way.
Do you think Elaine feels hurt that you told her you didn't want to play and to go away?

Dorothy: I guess so—maybe it was mean—but I just want to play alone for a while.

Connie: It's OK to want some time by yourself, but we have to think about how we say things to others. What do you think you could say to Elaine to make her feel better—maybe something like "Elaine, I like playing doctor with you, but right now I just want to play by myself. Maybe we could have snack together later." Does that sound like Elaine might feel OK about not playing doctor anymore?

Dorothy: Yes, maybe she'd feel better.

Connie: Can you say something like that to Elaine so she feels better and you are still friends?

Dorothy: Elaine, you are my friend I just want to be by myself now. We can have snack together, OK?

Elaine: OK, I'm glad you're still my friend. I'll go play with Jimmy. I can't wait for snack. I'm hungry!

Connie: I think you are both very caring to want to make Elaine's baby feel better and maybe later we can read books about doctors and nurses or maybe we'll read about Blue and her feelings. OK?

Extension Activity Chart

BOOK: *THE VERY HUNGRY CATERPILLAR*

Read-Aloud Techniques	Extension Activities	Children Learn
Talk about front cover: picture, title, author	Act out the caterpillar coming out of the egg, building a cocoon, and becoming a butterfly (*Scientific Thinking, Arts*)	**Concepts about print:** front and back cover, title, author
Connect: What do you do when you're hungry?		**Comprehension:** predicting, connecting story to their own experiences, using pictures
Predict: Do you think the caterpillar will eat a lot in this story? What do you think he will eat?	Retell with flannelboard what the caterpillar ate each day (*Mathematical Thinking, Language and Literacy*)	**Vocabulary:** tiny, cocoon, caterpillar, butterfly
Look at back cover	Explore five senses with the fruits. Example: Feel the skin of an orange, smell the orange when you cut it up, taste it for snack (*Scientific Thinking*)	**Numbers and counting**
Talk about the word "tiny" and how little the caterpillar looks in the picture		**Days of the week**
Count fruit together		**Colors**
Connect: eating too much and getting a stomachache	Talk about the Saturday eating binge (food groups, fact and fiction / real and make-believe: What do caterpillars really eat?) (*Scientific Thinking, Language and Literacy*)	**Healthy food choices**
Green leaf made the caterpillar feel better		**Fact vs. fiction**
Do you feel better when you eat healthy food?		**Five senses**
Talk about the big, fat caterpillar and look back at the "tiny" caterpillar	Build a cocoon or go on a nature walk (*Scientific Thinking*)	**Beginning understanding of the life cycle**
Props: stuffed caterpillar and butterfly	Use colored scarves and music to act out becoming a butterfly (*Arts*)	

Sample Fingerplay and Song

Fingerplay: *This Little Teddy*

This little teddy has a soft furry suit.

This little teddy is sweet and cute.

This little teddy is sassy and cross.

This little teddy thinks she's the boss.

This little teddy like berries and honey,

But when he gets them on his face,

He looks very, very funny.

Fingerplay: *Teddy Bear Teddy Bear Turn Around*

Teddy Bear Teddy Bear, turn around,

Teddy Bear Teddy Bear, touch the ground,

Teddy Bear Teddy Bear, reach up high,

Teddy Bear Teddy Bear, wink one eye,

Teddy Bear Teddy Bear, slap your knees,

Teddy Bear Teddy Bear, sit down please.

Song: *The Bear Went over the Mountain*

(to the tune of "For He's a Jolly Good Fellow")

The bear went over the mountain,

The bear went over the mountain,

The bear went over the mountain,

To see what he could see.

To see what he could see,

To see what he could see.

The bear went over the mountain,

To see what he could see.

The other side of the mountain,

The other side of the mountain,

The other side of the mountain,

Was all that he could see.

Was all that he could see,

Was all that he could see,

The other side of the mountain,

Was all that he could see!

Kindergarten Skills Matching Activity Answer Key

Gains meaning by listening

- Listening attentively to stories read aloud
- Listening to an audio-taped story or song and showing understanding through body language (clapping or nodding) or facial expressions (smiling or laughing)
- Using information from a story read aloud to draw a picture or complete a craft activity

Speaks clearly and conveys ideas effectively

- Asking a question clearly enough for someone to understand
- Describing a recent event and answering questions about it
- Speaking loudly enough to be heard by the whole group at a storytime session

Demonstrates beginning phonemic awareness

- Joining in with other children to recite rhymes and poems
- Experimenting with words; giving them new beginning sounds
- Listening to a word and then finding a word that rhymes with it in a familiar story, such as a Dr. Seuss story

Shows some understanding of concepts about print

- Finding the front of the book; turning the pages one by one
- Pointing to words in a left-to-right progression when "reading" a picture book
- Recognizing a favorite book by its cover; pointing to the title while saying it

Comprehends and responds to fiction and nonfiction text

- Guessing what will happen next by looking at the pictures on the following page
- Retelling a story using flannelboard cutouts or hand puppets
- Telling about when the family car was towed after hearing a story about a tow truck

Uses letterlike shapes, symbols, letters, and words to convey meaning

- Making rows of squiggles and shapes on a paper and calling it writing
- Copying letters or words from signs and books; enjoying the power of doing "real writing"
- Writing their names on their artwork

EMERGENT LITERACY NEWSLETTER

MONTH • YEAR

Alphabetic Principle: Fun with Letter Recognition and Letter Sounds

It is best to start building letter recognition with uppercase letters. Around the age of four, many preschoolers are ready to start learning about lowercase letters also. Always keep it fun, and judge your pace by the child's interest at their age!

Beginning Letter Recognition

- Make the child's name with magnetic letters on a cookie sheet. Name each letter and then call attention to the first letter. "S is for Sam!" Let your child play with the letters.
- Make a big S on a paper. Trace it with glue and then sprinkle it with glitter. Hang it on the wall. (You can also glue macaroni, beans, etc. to make a special picture.)
- Make a large letter on the floor with masking tape. Talk with your child about the name of the letter and a word that begins with the letter. Have the child walk or hop around the masking tape shape of the letter and say the letter name.

Advanced Letter Recognition

- Have fun making an alphabet caterpillar! Write each letter of the alphabet on a large construction paper circle. Mix the circles and spread them out on the table or floor. Work with the children to form the caterpillar by placing its body in alphabetical order. You can attach antennae to the "A" circle for the caterpillar's head. This is an activity that will be fun repeating!

Dear Workshop Participant:

We hope you are enjoying the many books and activities from the Ready At Five kit with your children. We are excited to also be able to send you two puppets to add to the fun as you and your children engage in prereading activities.

Puppets are fascinating to children. They know that puppets are not alive, yet they often listen to and talk with them as if they are real. Your puppets may be used in many ways to promote school readiness skills:

- Children can make up stories or retell stories read to them for you or other children (builds critical language, reading, and communication skills—oral language).
- Children can use their imagination and enjoy the puppets during make believe play.
- You can use a puppet to engage a child in conversations (opportunity to discuss their feelings, fears, anger, sharing).
- Have fun with puppets as children pretend to be the animal in songs or rhymes that you share (e.g., "Old MacDonald had a Farm" or "Three Little Pigs Blues" by Greg and Steve on their CD Playing Favorites, which is available from the library).
- Read fiction or nonfiction books together about the two animals your puppets represent (cow, bear, duck, pig, frog, etc.). Let your child pretend to be the animal while using the puppet.

We hope you found the parent reports on your children helpful as you continue to have fun with activities together. Here are some additional ideas to try for several of the areas of early literacy development.

- Cut out twenty-six fish shapes from construction paper and let your children decorate one side of the fish. On the other side print an uppercase letter of the alphabet. Slide a paper clip onto each fish's tail. Make a fishing rod by tying a string around the end of a dowel or stick. Then tie your magnet to the other end of the string. Scatter the fish, letter-side down, on the floor and let the children try to fish with their fishing rod. When they catch a fish, have them say the name of the letter on the other side of their fish. (For children a little more advanced, have them say the letter's sound and a word that starts with the same letter and sound.)

- Write your child's name at the top of a paper in large letters, using an uppercase letter for the first letter in your child's name, followed by the lowercase letters. Place your plastic letters that are in the child's name into a paper bag (be sure the first letter of the name is an uppercase letter in the bag). Also include one or two letters that are not part of your child's name. Ask your child to pick a letter out of the bag and look at it, and then look at his or her name. Ask if that letter is the his name. If it is in the name, ask the child to place it on the paper under the written letter and to tell you the name of the letter. Continue until your child has picked out all the letters in his or her name. (Depending on children's age and ability, they may be able to use a large crayon or pencil to try to begin writing their name on the paper.)

- Place ten of your plastic letters in a bag. Model the activity by closing your eyes and picking out a letter. As you feel the letter with your eyes closed, describe what letter you think you've picked. Open your eyes and confirm your answer with your child. Now, have your child pick a letter from the bag with eyes closed and ask "What letter do you think you've chosen?" If the child has trouble identifying the letter, give some clues.

Letters and Sounds

- You can expose children to the sounds of a few consonants when you think they are ready. For example, "B makes the /b/ sound. Banana, boat, bottle all start with b!"

- You can put objects in a pillowcase and pull them out one at a time. Have the names of the objects written on a few index cards. For example, "Let's see what we have in our mystery bag that starts with B. A book! B- B- Book! Book starts with a b." Give the child an index card with the word "book" written on it to place on the book.

- Attached are several sheets with examples of objects to use to help the children learn letter sounds. You can copy any of them and, if you'd like, you could use the set that is enlarged for the children to color while you talk about the letters and sounds. You could make a set of letters and a set of the pictures that go with each letter. Then you could choose four or five at a time for the children to match the picture of the letter sound object with the alphabet letter, for example the letter p with the picture of a pig. They could also make their own alphabet sound book by finding pictures in magazines of the objects that show the sound for each letter. You would write the letter on each page for them.

Comprehension:
Understanding What Is Happening in a Story

When you are going to read a book for the first time to the children, look through the story and put sticky notes on a couple of places where it would be good to stop and ask "What do you think might happen next?" Try to pick obvious places where something is surely going to happen.

Again, if you feel the children aren't quite ready for this, just do it yourself and model for them at first. For example, "I would feel sad and upset if someone took my things without asking, wouldn't you? Let's see what the boy in the story tells his friend."

Pick a couple of places in the story to ask "what" or "how" questions that help the children connect the story to their own lives. For example, "What would you do if that happened to you?" or "How do you feel when someone takes one of your toys without asking?"

If you feel the child or children are not quite ready for this, just do it yourself and model for them. For example, "Oh, this is a good part! I think the bears will be mad when they find out what Goldilocks has done, don't you? Let's read and find out!"

Message from the Project Director

I do hope that you all will enjoy and find this newsletter useful—along with the two puppets! I also want to thank you for your participation in the first training workshop. If you haven't heard from me yet, I will be calling everyone before to ask how things are going in regard to applying the training to your regular activities. I will be looking for one or two thoughts from you to include in our next newsletter. Have a wonderful Holiday season!

Name

Title

Library

Phone/email

Some winter picture books you might enjoying sharing with your children. They are available at library branches or you may request them through the day care van service.

Snow Day by Patricia Lakin
If I Had a Snowplow by Jean L. S. Patrick
Snowballs by Lois Ehlert
All You Need for a Snowman by Alice Schertle
Mouse's First Snow by Lauren Thompson
Hello Snow by Hope Vestergaard
Snowmen at Night by Caralyn Buchner
A Perfect Day for It by Jan Fearnley
Bear Snores On by Karma Wilson
Dinos in the Snow by Karma Wilson
First Snow by Bernette Ford
A Hat for Minerva Louise by Janet Morgan Stoeke
There Was a Cold Lady Who Swallowed Some Snow by Lucille Colandro
Biscuit's Snowy Day by Alyssa Satin Capucilli
Zoopa: An Animal Alphabet by Gianna Marino

Early Literacy School Readiness Follow-up Workshop Sample Agenda

9:00–9:05:

I. Introductions/housekeeping/collect survey. *Librarian*

9:05–9:15:

II. Review training goals. *Librarian*

9:15–10:05:

III. Sharing session. *Participants, librarian as facilitator*

10:05–10:20:

IV. Snapshots.[†] *Librarian*

10:20–10:45:

V. Print awareness—promote books. *Librarian*

10:45–11:00:

VI. Evaluation and closing; include peer coaching/feedback reminder and certificates of completion.[†]

[†] Can be found on the ALA Editions Web Extras website, www.alaeditions.org/webextras.

Sample Participants' Comments

Comments from Phone Conversations

- Having new things to use from the activity kit is motivating the children and motivating me, too.

- I used sidewalk chalk to make a big game board grid of shapes on the driveway and drew every shape its own color, so that the little ones who know their colors could participate even if they did not know their shapes yet.

Comments about the Newsletters

- They have definitely rejuvenated me with ideas and excitement! Newsletters have continued to reinforce ways we can teach reading in day-to-day activities. Music is now a daily activity due to great resources.

- The children love the puppets that came with the newsletter. Besides reading storybooks, I use puppets to tell little made-up stories. The children now ask, "Will you tell me a story from your head?"

Comments in a Follow-up Workshop

- Children call the blue box of supplies "the magic box" and use it all the time to come up with activities.

- Did the Sink or Float science activity—even older children (elementary school age) were engaged and surprised when some of their guesses did not do what they predicted.

Learning in Early Childhood, Brain Development

Bergen, Doris. "The Role of Pretend Play in Children's Cognitive Development." *Early Childhood Research and Practice* 4, no. 1 (2002), http://ecrp.uiuc.edu/v4n1/bergen.html.

Brazelton, T. Berry. *Touchpoints Three to Six: Your Child's Emotional and Behavior Development.* Cambridge, MA: Perseus Publications, 2001.

———. *Touchpoints Birth to Three: Your Child's Emotional and Behavior Development.* Cambridge, MA: Da Capo Press: 2006.

Caine, R. N., and G. Caine. *Making Connections: Teaching and the Human Brain.* Menlo Park, CA: Addison-Wesley, 1991.

Calkins, Susan, and Amanda P. Willford. *Handbook of Child Development and Early Education: Research to Practice.* New York: Guildford Press, 2009.

Cecchini, Marie E. "How Dramatic Play Can Enhance Learning." Early Childhood News, 2008. www.earlychildhoodnews.com/earlychildhood/article_view.aspx?ArticleID=751.

Center on the Social and Emotional Foundations for Early Learning (CSEFEL). http://csefel.vanderbilt.edu.

Dewar, Gwen. "The Cognitive Benefits of Play: Effects on the Learning Brain." Parenting Science, 2008, www.parentingscience.com/benefits-of-play.html.

Donovan, Suzanne, and M. Susan Burns. *Eager to Learn: Educating Our Preschoolers*. Washington, DC: National Academies Press, 2001.

Goodwin, Susan, and Linda Acredolo. *Baby Hearts: A Guide to Giving Your Child an Emotional Head Start*. New York: Bantam, 2005.

Hirsch-Pasek, Kathy. *Einstein Didn't Use Flashcards! How Our Children Really Learn and Why They Need to Play More and Memorize Less*. New York: Rodale Press, 2003.

Lenroot, Rhoshel K., and Jay N. Giedd. "Brain Development in Children and Adolescents: Insights from Anatomical Magnetic Resonance Imaging." *Neuroscience and Biobehavioral Reviews* 30, no. 6 (2006): 718–729.

Medina, John. *Brain Rules for Baby: How to Raise a Smart and Happy Child from Zero to Five*. Seattle, WA: Pear Press, 2010.

Myers-Walls, Judith. "Children and Learning." *Provider-Parent Partnerships*. Purdue University. www.ces.purdue.edu/providerparent/Children-Learning/main-CL.htm.

National Institute for Early Education Research. "Looking at Play the Healthy Way: Imaginative Play Helps Teach Self-Regulation Skills." *Preschool Matters* 6, no. 2 (2008): 3–5.

Neuman, Susan B. "N Is for Nonsensical." *Educational Leadership*, October 2006, 28–31.

Neuman, Susan B., and Donna Celano. "Books Aloud: A Campaign to Put Books in Children's Hands." *Reading Teacher* 54, no. 6 (March 2001): 550–557.

Paulu, Nancy. "Helping Your Child Get Ready for School." KidSource OnLine, 1992. www.kidsource.com/kidsource/content/getready.html.

Shonkoff, Jack P., and Deborah A. Phillips, eds. *From Neurons to Neighborhoods: The Science of Early Childhood Development*. Washington, DC: National Academies Press, 2000.

Singer, Dorothy G., Roberta Golinkoff, and Kathy Hirsch-Pasek, eds. *Play = Learning: How Play Motivates and Enhances Children's Cognitive and Social Emotional Growth*. New York: Oxford University Press, 2006.

Smith, Peter K., and Craig H. Hart, eds. *Blackwell Handbook of Childhood Social Development*. Oxford: Blackwell, 2002.

U.S. Department of Education. "Early Childhood Growth Chart—Language." KidSource OnLine. www.kidsource.com/kidsource/content4/growth.chart/page1html.

Wells, Rosemary. *My Shining Star: Raising a Child Who Is Ready to Learn*. New York: Scholastic Press, 2006.

Zero to Three. "Brain Development." www.zerotothree.org/child-development/brain-development.

Zigler, Edward F., Dorothy G. Singer, and Sandra J. Bishop-Josef, eds. *Children's Play: The Roots of Reading*. Washington, DC: Zero to Three Press, 2004.

Libraries, Community Partners, and School Readiness

Brickmayer, Jennifer. "The Role of Public Libraries in Emergent and Family Literacy." *Zero to Three* 21, no. 3 (2001): 25–30.

Crowther, Janet L., and Barry Trott. *Partnering with a Purpose: A Guide to Strategic Partnership Development for Libraries and Other Organizations*. Englewood, CA: Libraries Unlimited, 2004.

Czarnecki, Elaine M., Dorothy Stoltz, and Connie Wilson. "Every Child Was Ready to Learn." *Public Libraries* 47, no. 3 (2008): 45–51.

Diamant-Cohen, Betsy, ed. *Children's Services: Partnerships for Success*. Chicago: American Library Association, 2010.

———. *Early Literacy Programming en Español*. New York: Neal-Schuman, 2010.

Diamant-Cohen, Betsy, and Saroj Nadkarni Ghoting. *The Early Literacy Kit: A Handbook and Tip Cards*. Chicago: American Library Association, 2010.

Dresang, Eliza T., and Kathleen Campana. *Emergent Readers Literacy Training and Assessment Program: Research Report*. (Unpublished report prepared for the Pierce County [WA] Library System.) 2011. www.piercecountylibrary.org/files/library/research-report.pdf.

Every Child Ready to Read @ your library. 2nd ed. www.everychildreadytoread.org/project-history%09/literature-review-2010. See also http://everychildreadytoread.ning.com.

Felman, Sari, and Barbara Jordan. "Together Is Better: The Role of Libraries as Natural Community Partners." *Zero to Three* 21, no. 3 (2001): 30–37.

Getting Ready. "School Readiness Indicators Initiative." www.gettingready.org.

Ghoting, Saroj Nadkarni, and Pamela Martin-Díaz. *Early Literacy Storytimes @ your library: Partnering with Caregivers for Success*. Chicago: American Library Association, 2006.

Martinez, Gilda. "Libraries, Families, and Schools: Partnership to Achieve School Reading Readiness; A Multiple Case Study of Maryland Public Librarians." *Children and Libraries* 5, no. 1 (2007): 32–39.

———. "Public Libraries: Community Organizations Making Outreach Efforts to Help Young Children Succeed in School." *School Community Journal* 18, no. 1 (2008): 93–104.

Mediavilla, Cindy, and Natalie Cole. "We Read Together: Los Angeles Public Library Early Literacy Parent/Caregiver Workshop Evaluation." Unpublished report prepared for the Los Angeles Public Library, 2012. Downloadable from http://everychildreadytoread.ning.com/page/research-3.

Minkel, Walter. "It's Never Too Early." *School Library Journal* 48, no. 7 (2002): 38–42, available at www.schoollibraryjournal.com/article/CA225245.html.

Parlakian, Rebecca. *Before the ABCs: Promoting School Readiness in Infants and Toddlers*. Washington, DC: Zero to Three Press, 2003.

Reading Rockets. "For Preschool and Childcare." www.readingrockets.org/audience/professionals/preschool.

Ready At Five. "Parent Tips." www.readyatfive.org/raf/for-parents/parent-tips.html.

Reif, Kathleen. "Are Public Libraries the Preschooler's Door to Learning?" *Public Libraries* 39, no. 5 (2000): 262–265.

School Improvement in Maryland. "Early Childhood Initiatives," under Maryland Model for School Readiness. http://mdk12.org/instruction/ensure/readiness/index.html.

Snell, Kim. "Beyond Library Walls: Improving Kindergarten Readiness in At-Risk Communities." *Children and Libraries* 10, no. 1 (2012): 27–29.

Snow, Catherine E., M. Susan Burns, and Peg Griffin, eds. *Preventing Reading Difficulties in Young Children*. Washington, DC: National Academies Press, 1998.

———, eds. *Starting Out Right: A Guide to Promoting Children's Reading Success*. Washington, DC: National Academies Press, 1999.

Squires, Tasha. *Library Partnerships: Making Connections between School and Public Libraries*. Medford, OR: Information Today, 2009.

Stoltz, Dorothy, Elaine M. Czarnecki, Connie Wilson, and Gilda Martinez. "Improving Storytime Delivery with Peer Coaching." *Public Libraries* 49, no. 2 (2010): 44–49.

West Bloomfield Township Public Library. "Grow Up Reading." www.growupreading.org.

Whitehurst, Grover J. (Russ). "Dialogic Reading: An Effective Way to Read to Preschoolers." Reading Rockets, 1992. www.readingrockets.org/article/400.

Organizing, Managing, and Promoting Early Childhood Outreach Initiatives

Carolina Abecedarian Project. www.fpg.unc.edu/~abc/.

Heckman, James J. "Invest in the Very Young." Ounce of Prevention Fund, 2000. www.ounceofprevention.org/news/pdfs/HeckmanInvestInVeryYoung.pdf.

HighScope. "HighScope Perry Preschool Study." www.highscope.org/content.asp?contentid=219.

Isaacs, Julia B. "Cost Effective Investments in Children." Brookings Institution, 2007. www.brookings.edu/views/papers/200701isaacs.pdf.

National Association for the Education of Young Children. "Research Studies and Task Force Reports Can Help You Advocate for High-Quality Early Childhood Education." www.naeyc.org/files/naeyc/ResearchStudies.pdf.

OCLC WebJunction. "Communication and Partnership—Tools." www.webjunction .org/maintainit-cookbooks/-/articles/content/36821786.

Pinnicle Management. "Pareto Principle: How the 80/20 Rule Helps Us Be More Effective." www.pinnicle.com/Articles/Pareto_Principle/pareto_principle.html.

Reynolds, Arthur J., Judy Temle, Dylan L. Robertson, and Emily A. Mann. "Age 21 Cost-Benefit Analysis of the Title 1 Chicago Child-Parent Center Program: Executive Summary," 2001. www.waisman.wisc.edu/cls/cbaexecsum4.html.

Sniderman, Mark S. "Stop Investing in Stadiums . . . Start Investing in Kids: An Interview with Art Rolnick." Federal Reserve Bank of Cleveland, June 10, 2010. www.clevelandfed.org/Forefront/2010/09/ff_2010_fall_05.cfm.

Index

You may also be interested in

Transforming Preschool Storytime
A Modern Vision and a Year of Programs

BETSY DIAMANT-COHEN AND MELANIE A. HETRICK

Here is a new approach to storytime that incorporates more recent theories on developmental learning and research on how children's brains work.

ISBN: 978-1-55570-805-4
336 PAGES / 6" x 9"

LISTENING TO LEARN
Audiobooks Supporting Literacy
SHARON GROVER AND
LIZETTE D. HANNEGAN
ISBN: 978-0-8389-1107-5

FUNDAMENTALS OF CHILDREN'S SERVICES, SECOND EDITION
MICHAEL SULLIVAN
ISBN: 978-0-8389-1188-4

THE EARLY LITERACY KIT
A Handbook and Tip Cards
BETSY DIAMANT-COHEN AND
SAROJ NADKARNI GHOTING
ISBN: 978-0-8389-0999-7

COTEACHING READING COMPREHENSION STRATEGIES IN ELEMENTARY SCHOOL LIBRARIES
JUDI MOREILLON
ISBN: 978-0-8389-1180-8

BOOKS IN MOTION
Connecting Preschoolers with Books through Art, Games, Movement, Music, Playacting, and Props
JULIE DIETZEL-GLAIR
ISBN: 978-1-55570-810-8

FROM CHILDREN'S LITERATURE TO READERS THEATRE
ELIZABETH A. POE
ISBN: 978-0-8389-1049-8

Order today at **alastore.ala.org** or **866-746-7252!**

ALA Store purchases fund advocacy, awareness, and accreditation programs for library professionals worldwide.